Seasonal Activities

Activities to reinforce basic skills,
for enrichment or just plain fun!

- Crossword Puzzles
- Write Poetry
- Story Starters
- Word Search

- Dot-to-Dot
- Jigsaw Puzzles
- And More...

Fall Activities...............page 3 - 50

Winter Activities.......page 51 - 98

Spring Activities.......page 99 - 153

Summer Activities......page 154 - 208

Fall
Activities

Seasonal Activities

Name It!

	something in your house	parts of your body	a fruit or vegetable	a city or state	an animal with 4 legs
example T	table	toe	turnip	Texas	turtle
F					
A					
L					
L					

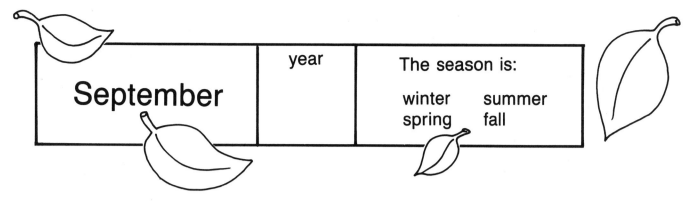

September	year	The season is: winter summer spring fall

Sunday	Monday	Tuesday	Wednesday	Thursday	Friday	Saturday

1. Write the number for each day in September.
2. There are always _____ days in September.
3. There are _____ Mondays in September.
4. Color the first day of school red.
5. Draw an autumn leaf on the first day of fall.
6. Record class birthdays on your calendar.

Turn this paper over and make a picture showing how you came to school on the first day (bicycle, car ...).

        Seasonal Activities

October	year	The season is: winter summer spring fall

Sunday	Monday	Tuesday	Wednesday	Thursday	Friday	Saturday

1. Write the number for each day in October.
2. There are always _____ days in October.
3. Name the days of the week you go to school.
4. Draw a boat on Columbus Day.
5. Make a black cat on Halloween.
6. Record class birthdays on your calendar.

Turn this paper over and show which Halloween creature you would choose to be.

November	year	The season is: winter summer spring fall	

Sunday	Monday	Tuesday	Wednesday	Thursday	Friday	Saturday

1. Write the number for each day in November.
2. There are always _____ days in November.
3. Which day is the first day of the week? _____
   Which day is the last day of the week? _____
4. Color each Saturday yellow and each Sunday green.
5. Draw a Pilgrim's hat on Thanksgiving Day.
6. Record class birthdays on your calendar.

Turn this paper over and draw a picture of the first Thanksgiving feast.

Back to School Puzzle

Across
2. a work table at school
4. you can write with this
5. an instructor
7. you read a _____
8. a group of students
10. to put words on paper
11. what you do at recess
12. a mealtime
14. a place to check out books to take home

Down
1. playtime at school
3. a place to go to learn
4. the head of the school
6. a place to eat lunch
7. a vehicle that carries children to school
9. to do lessons
10. lessons you do at home are called home _____
13. report _____

Word Box

lunch	cafeteria	work	pencil	study	desk
card	library	play	book	write	bus
teacher	school	class	recess	principal	

Seasonal Activities

Circle each word in the puzzle as you find it.
You will find words across, down and diagonally.
A few words are written backwards.

School Days

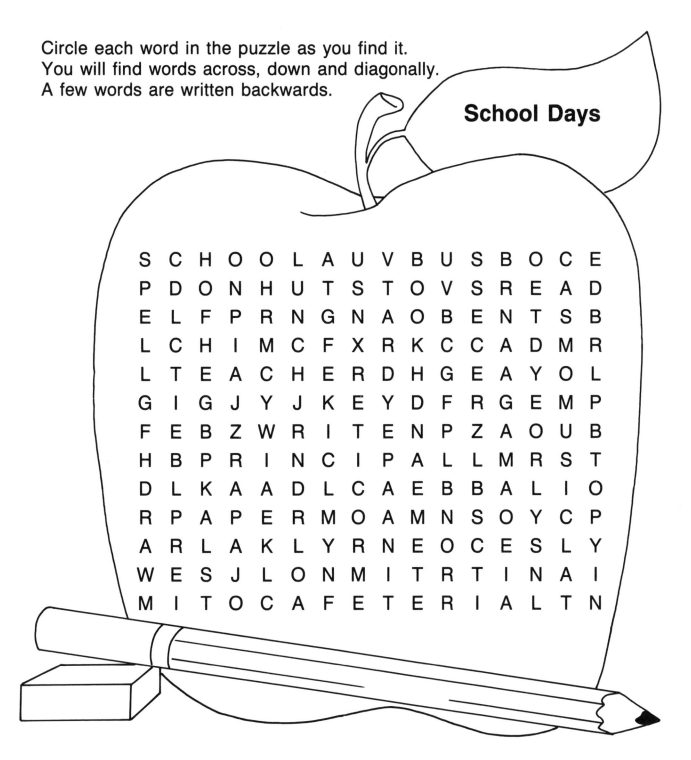

```
S C H O O L A U V B U S B O C E
P D O N H U T S T O V S R E A D
E L F P R N G N A O B E N T S B
L C H I M C F X R K C C A D M R
L T E A C H E R D H G E A Y O L
G I G J Y J K E Y D F R G E M P
F E B Z W R I T E N P Z A O U B
H B P R I N C I P A L L M R S T
D L K A A D L C A E B B A L I O
R P A P E R M O A M N S O Y C P
A R L A K L Y R N E O C E S L Y
W E S J L O N M I T R T I N A I
M I T O C A F E T E R I A L T N
```

Cross out each word as you find it.

read	book	school
recess	bus	library
spell	cafeteria	lunch
tardy	paper	music
teacher	pencil	draw
write	play	gym
absent	principal	learn

Seasonal Activities

Which words go together?

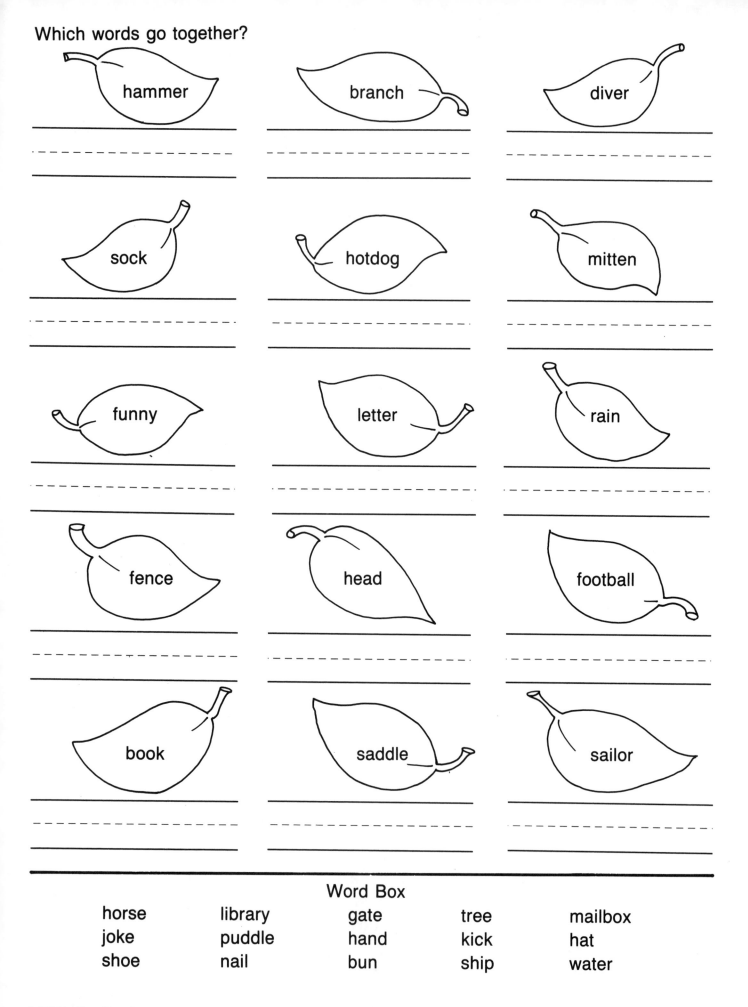

hammer

branch

diver

sock

hotdog

mitten

funny

letter

rain

fence

head

football

book

saddle

sailor

Word Box

horse	library	gate	tree	mailbox
joke	puddle	hand	kick	hat
shoe	nail	bun	ship	water

Seasonal Activities

Fall Cinquain

by _____

One word _____
(title)

Two Words _____
(describe)

Three Words _____
(action)

Four Words _____
(feeling)

One Word _____
(refer back to title)

1. Cut out pictures.　2. Paste to lined paper.　3. Write.

Seasonal Activities

A Fall Crossword Puzzle

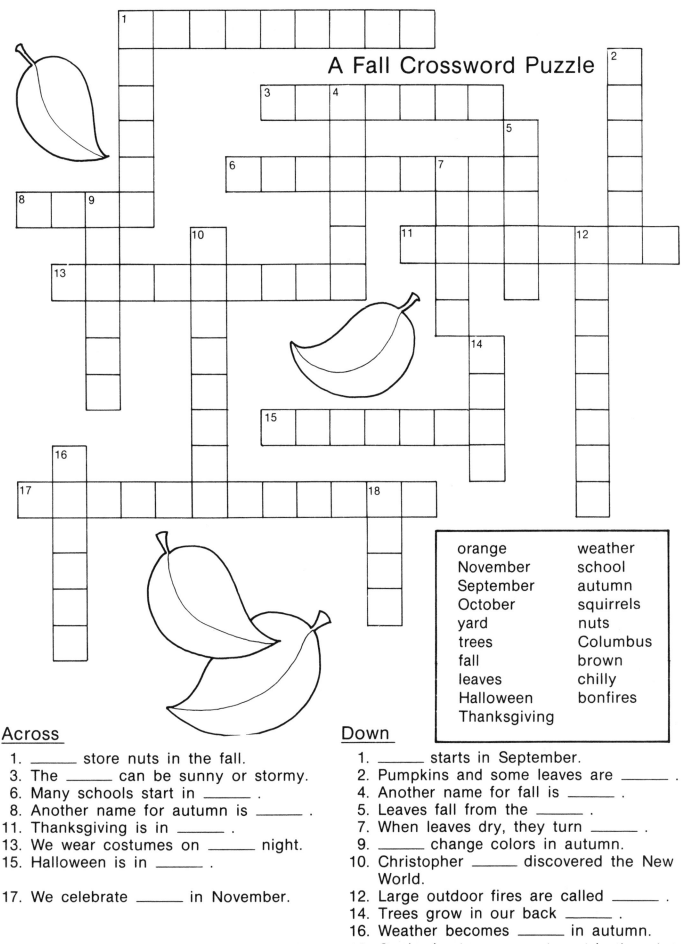

orange
November
September
October
yard
trees
fall
leaves
Halloween
Thanksgiving

weather
school
autumn
squirrels
nuts
Columbus
brown
chilly
bonfires

Across

1. _____ store nuts in the fall.
3. The _____ can be sunny or stormy.
6. Many schools start in _____ .
8. Another name for autumn is _____ .
11. Thanksgiving is in _____ .
13. We wear costumes on _____ night.
15. Halloween is in _____ .

17. We celebrate _____ in November.

Down

1. _____ starts in September.
2. Pumpkins and some leaves are _____ .
4. Another name for fall is _____ .
5. Leaves fall from the _____ .
7. When leaves dry, they turn _____ .
9. _____ change colors in autumn.
10. Christopher _____ discovered the New World.
12. Large outdoor fires are called _____ .
14. Trees grow in our back _____ .
16. Weather becomes _____ in autumn.
18. Squirrels store _____ to eat in the winter.

Seasonal Activities

Columbus and his men traveled to America on sailing ships.

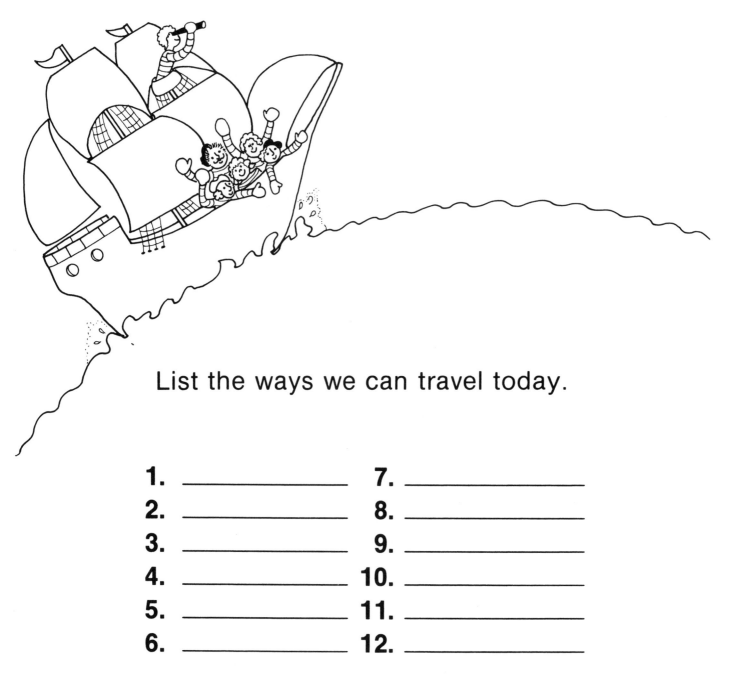

List the ways we can travel today.

1. _____   7. _____
2. _____   8. _____
3. _____   9. _____
4. _____   10. _____
5. _____   11. _____
6. _____   12. _____

Get a sheet of drawing paper.
Illustrate your favorite way to travel
or a new way you would like to try.

 Seasonal Activities

The Santa Maria

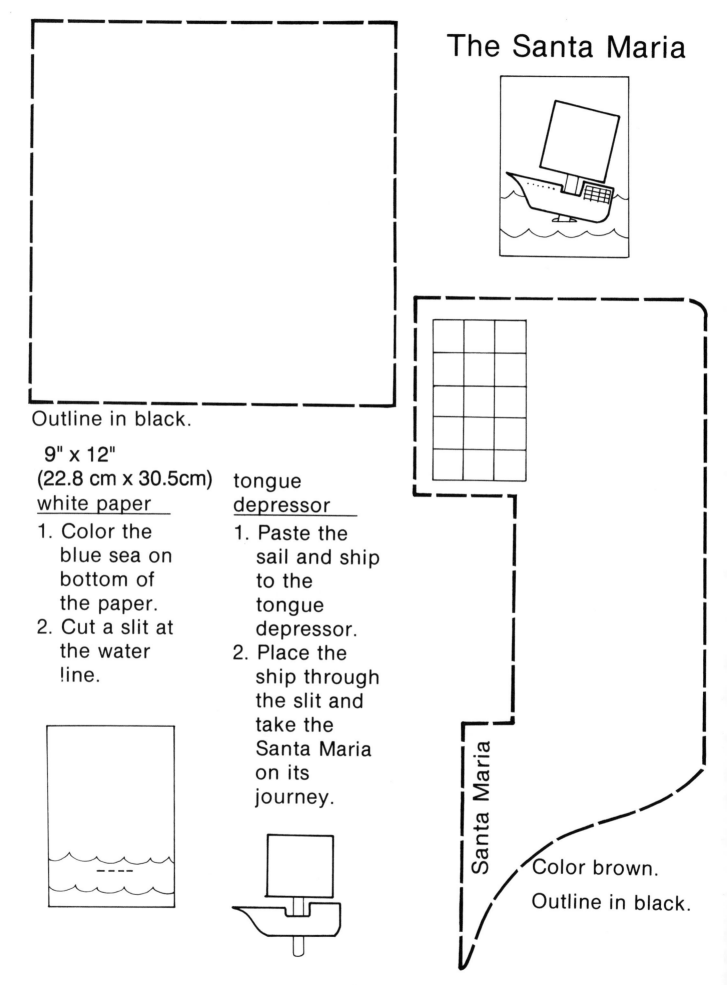

Outline in black.

**9" x 12"
(22.8 cm x 30.5cm)
white paper**

1. Color the blue sea on bottom of the paper.
2. Cut a slit at the water line.

tongue depressor

1. Paste the sail and ship to the tongue depressor.
2. Place the ship through the slit and take the Santa Maria on its journey.

Santa Maria

Color brown.

Outline in black.

Trace Christopher Columbus' voyage to the New World. Begin at Palos, Spain. Follow the dotted line to New World.

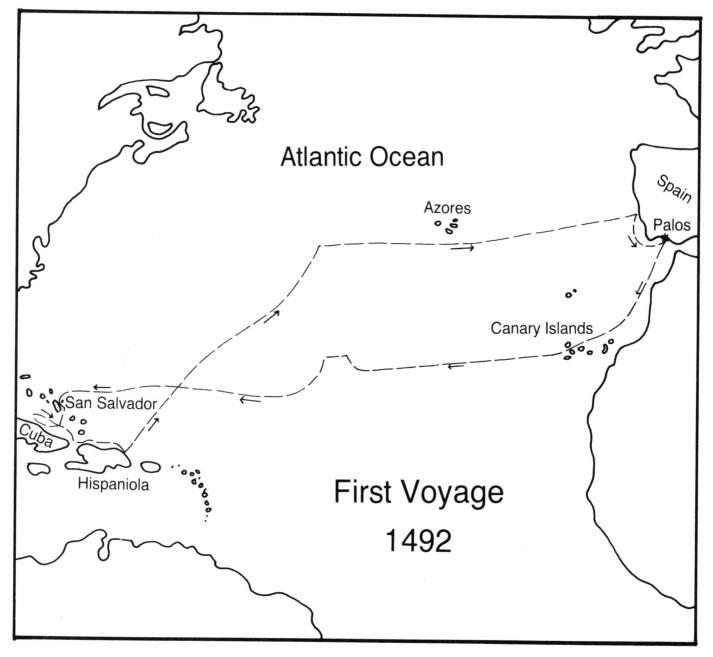

Atlantic Ocean

Azores

Spain

Palos

Canary Islands

San Salvador

Cuba

Hispaniola

First Voyage
1492

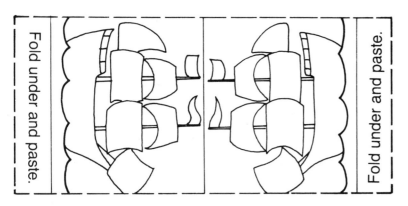

Fold under and paste.

Fold under and paste.

Color, cut, fold, paste.
Name your ship the Niña, Pinta, or Santa Maria.
Sail your ship along Columbus' route on the map above.

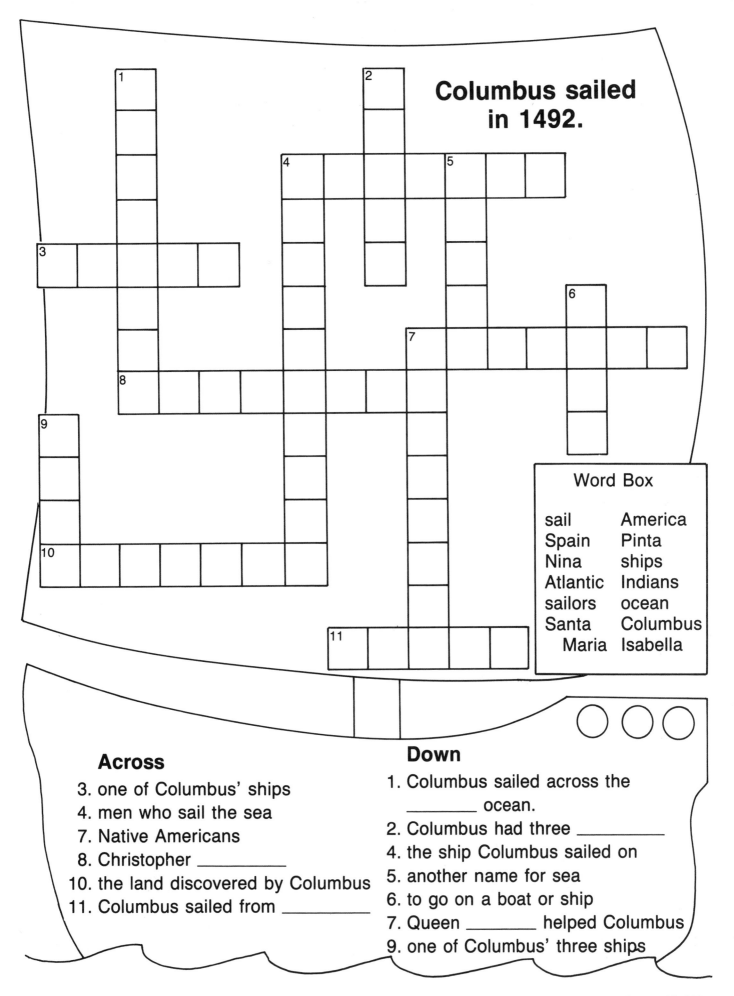

Columbus sailed in 1492.

Word Box

sail	America
Spain	Pinta
Nina	ships
Atlantic	Indians
sailors	ocean
Santa	Columbus
Maria	Isabella

Across

3. one of Columbus' ships
4. men who sail the sea
7. Native Americans
8. Christopher _____
10. the land discovered by Columbus
11. Columbus sailed from _____

Down

1. Columbus sailed across the _____ ocean.
2. Columbus had three _____
4. the ship Columbus sailed on
5. another name for sea
6. to go on a boat or ship
7. Queen _____ helped Columbus
9. one of Columbus' three ships

Seasonal Activities

Halloween Dreams

Put this picture together to find a Halloween surprise.

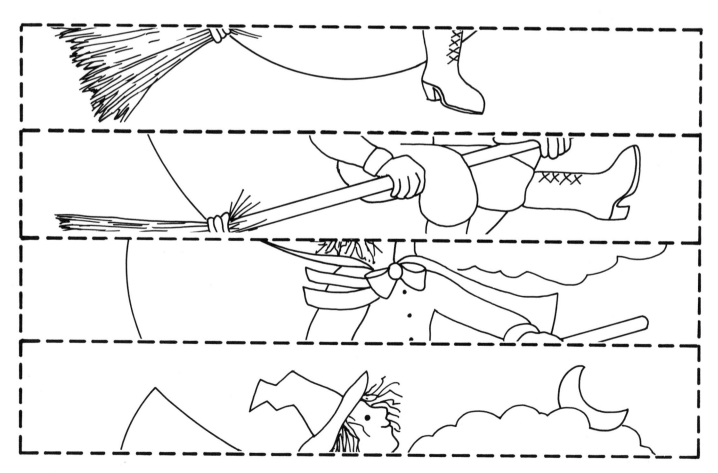

Drawing Fun

Who is sitting on the witch's broomstick?
Follow the steps and draw the surprise in the box.

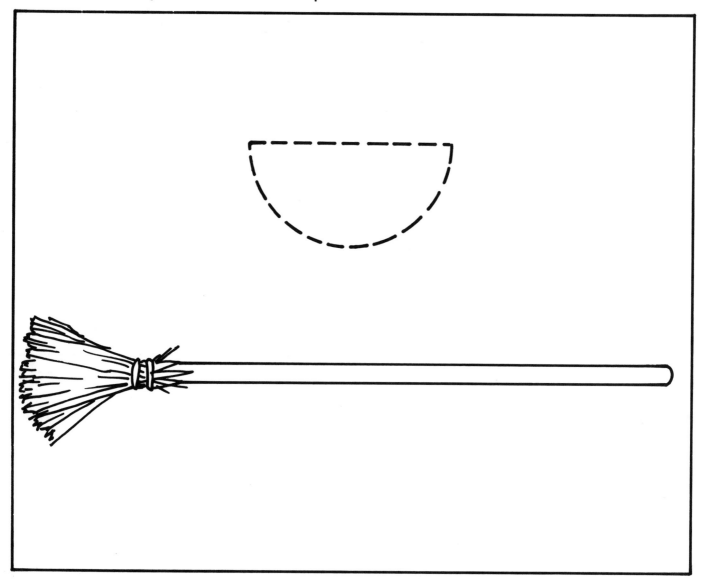

1. Follow the drawing steps.

2. Color the cat black with green eyes. Make the broomstick brown.

3. Add a big yellow moon.

20

Synonyms

penny

_____

- - - - - - - - - - - - -

_____

carton

_____

- - - - - - - - - - - - -

_____

leap

_____

- - - - - - - - - - - - -

_____

cushion

_____

- - - - - - - - - - - - -

_____

purse

_____

- - - - - - - - - - - - -

_____

bun

_____

- - - - - - - - - - - - -

_____

snapshot

_____

- - - - - - - - - - - - -

_____

rock

_____

- - - - - - - - - - - - -

_____

huge

_____

- - - - - - - - - - - - -

_____

trip

_____

- - - - - - - - - - - - -

_____

story

_____

- - - - - - - - - - - - -

_____

pitcher

_____

- - - - - - - - - - - - -

_____

quilt

_____

- - - - - - - - - - - - -

gown

_____

- - - - - - - - - - - - -

_____

canine

_____

- - - - - - - - - - - - -

_____

Word Box

roll	dress	cent	handbag	journey
large	pillow	boulder	box	jug
dog	photograph	bedspread	tale	jump

Seasonal Activities

1. Cut.   2. Paste to lined paper.   3. Write.

How to Grow
a
Pumpkin

How to Make
a
Jack o' Lantern

How to Eat
a
Pumpkin Pie

Seasonal Activities

1. Color 2. Cut out 3. Paste in order

1	2	3
4	5	6

I can pick the big, orange pumpkin.

See the plant grow.

A little pumpkin starts to grow.

Pumpkin flowers grow on the vine.

Plant the seeds.

Now I have a jack o lantern.

Seasonal Activities

The Name Game

Select a letter.

Each answer must begin with that letter.

1. What is your name?
2. Where do you live?
3. What do you eat?
4. What is your job?
5. What do you like to play?

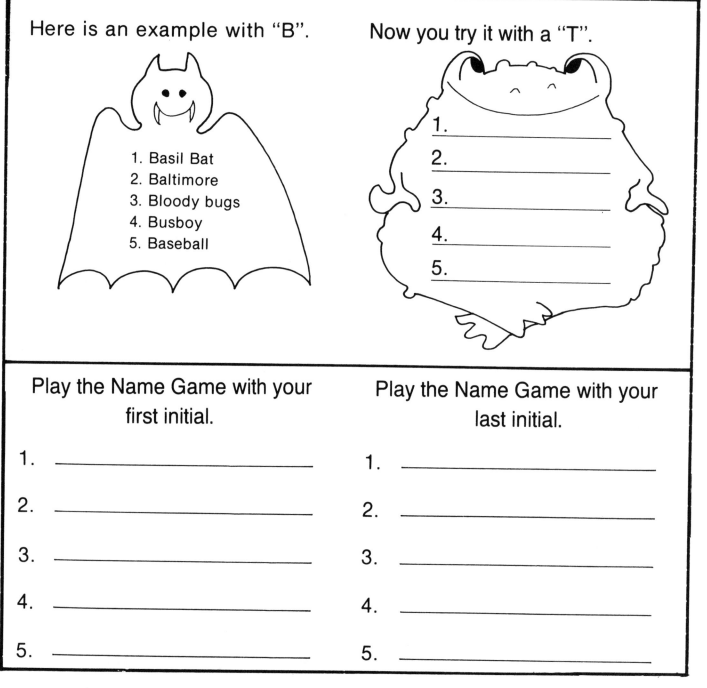

Here is an example with "B".

1. Basil Bat
2. Baltimore
3. Bloody bugs
4. Busboy
5. Baseball

Now you try it with a "T".

1. _____
2. _____
3. _____
4. _____
5. _____

Play the Name Game with your first initial.

1. _____
2. _____
3. _____
4. _____
5. _____

Play the Name Game with your last initial.

1. _____
2. _____
3. _____
4. _____
5. _____

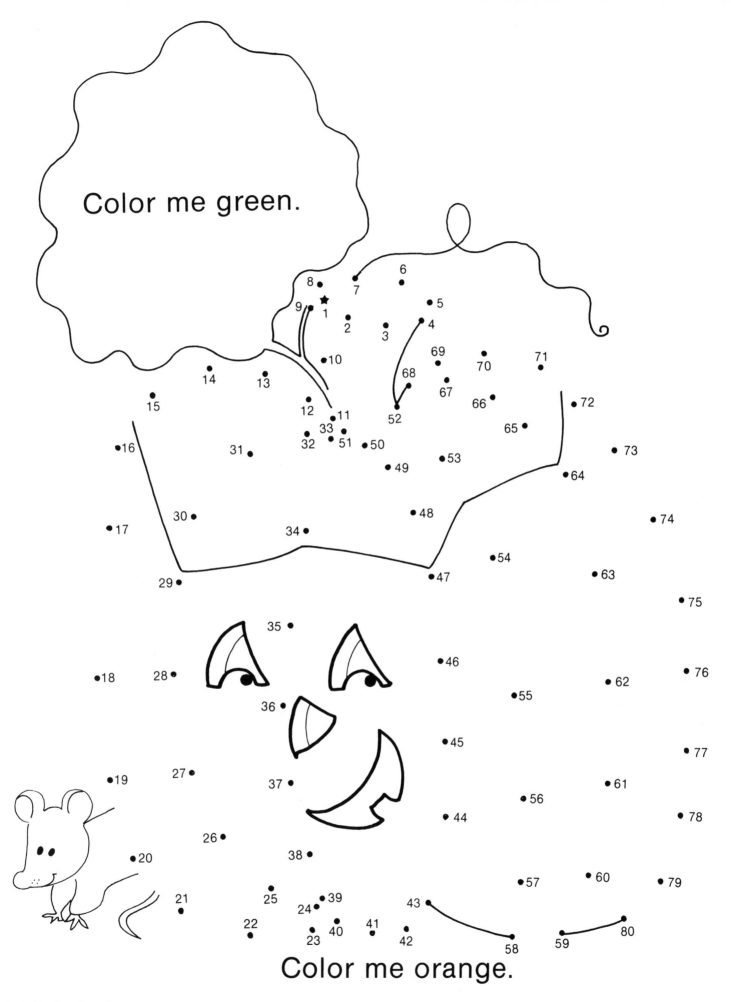

Color me green.

Color me orange.

Seasonal Activities

Crazy Creatures
A Flip Book

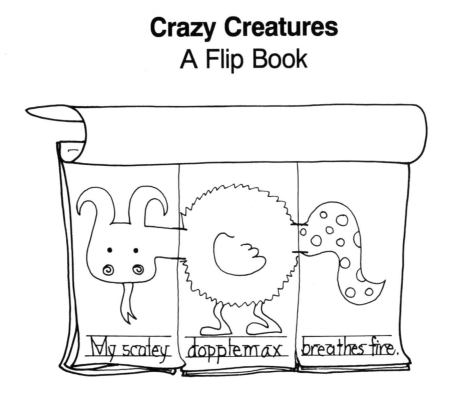

My scaley | dopplemax | breathes fire.

Step 1:   Draw the head, body and tail of your creature.
Be sure the neck touches point A and the tail
touches point B.

Step 2:   Box 1—*describe* your creature
an orange, bumpy...
a soft, slimey...

Box 2—*name* your creature
Glox
Sniggledorf

Box 3—tell what your creature *can do*
...eats wet garbage
...squashes tall buildings

Step 3:   Carefully cut the dotted lines on your page.
Don't cut too far!

Step 4:   Give the creature to your teacher.

Seasonal Activities

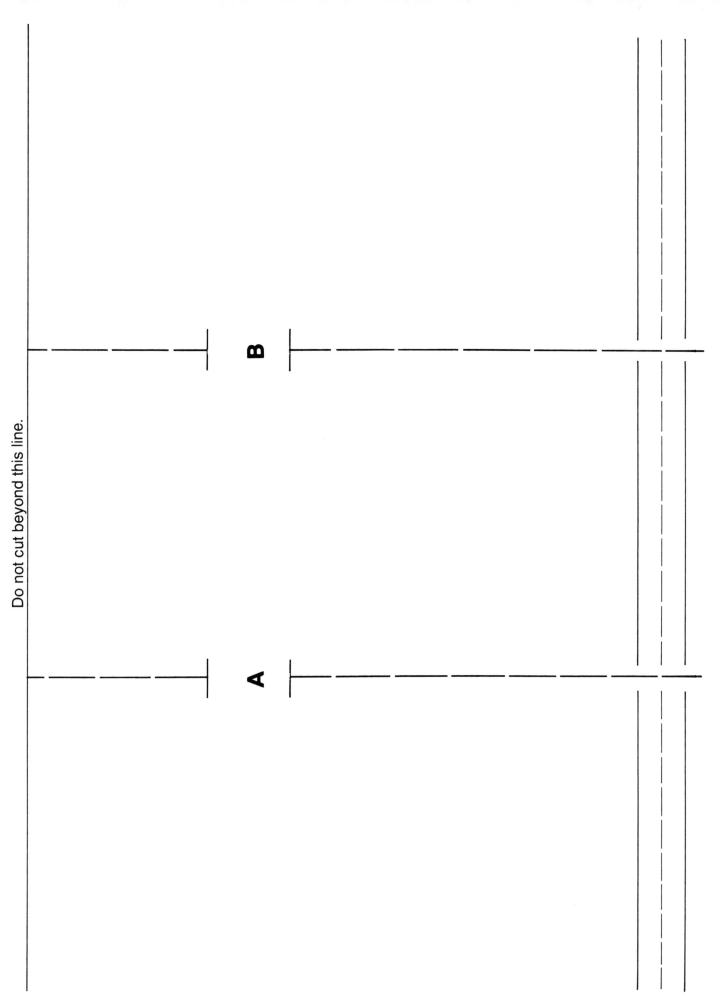

Do not cut beyond this line.

B

A

Find the "spooky" mystery word.

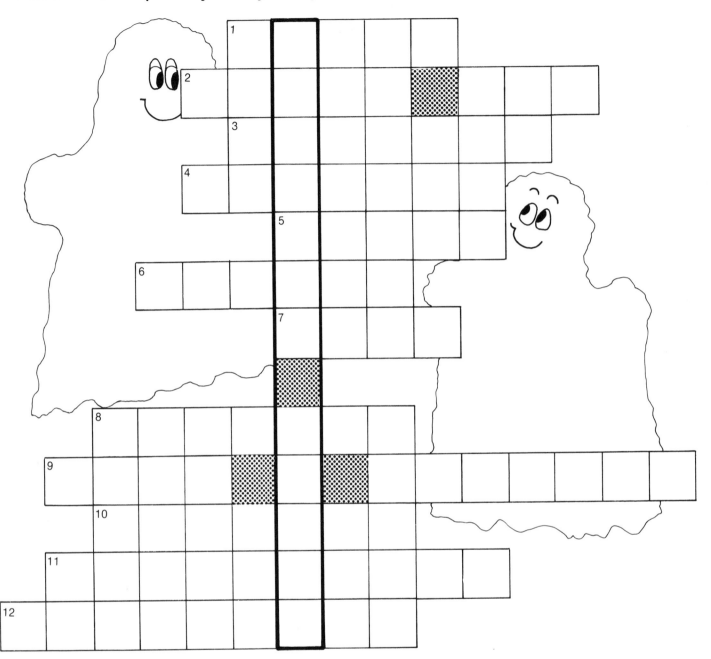

1. this spirit haunts houses
2. a witch's pet
3. round and orange; grows in a patch
4. a scary creature
5. trick or _____
6. a loud noise made when you are frightened
7. at night the sky is _____
8. they create magic spells
9. a pumpkin face
10. a disguise for Halloween
11. a witch rides on a _____
12. a night to dress in scary costumes

Draw the mystery picture on the back of this page.

Word box:
pumpkin
scream
jack o'lantern
Halloween
black cat
treat
witches
broomstick
ghost
monster
dark
costume

Seasonal Activities

HALLOWEEN WORD SEARCH

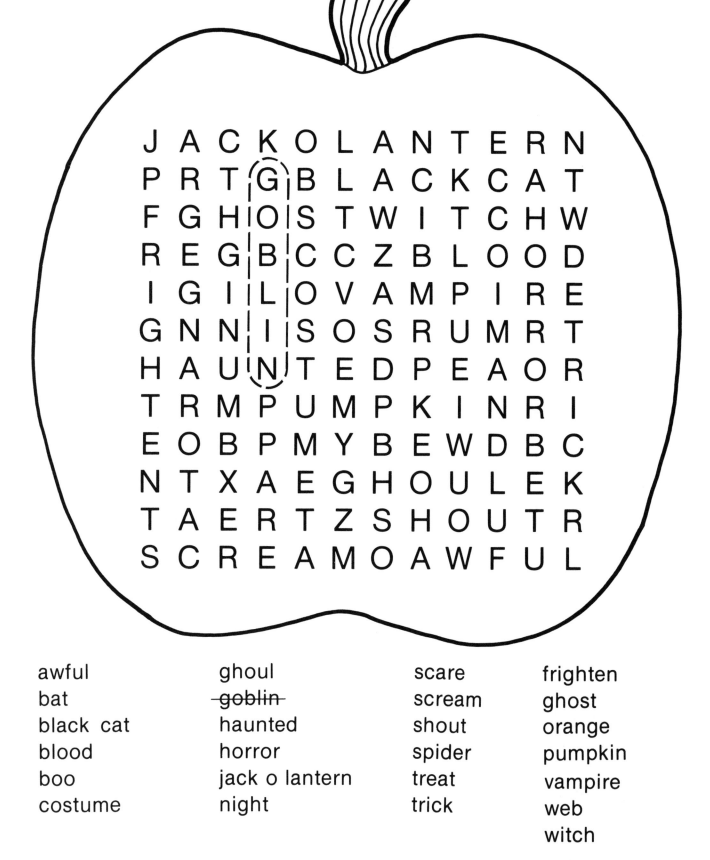

```
J A C K O L A N T E R N
P R T G B L A C K C A T
F G H O S T W I T C H W
R E G B C C Z B L O O D
I G I L O V A M P I R E
G N N I S O S R U M R T
H A U N T E D P E A O R
T R M P U M P K I N R I
E O B P M Y B E W D B C
N T X A E G H O U L E K
T A E R T Z S H O U T R
S C R E A M O A W F U L
```

awful	ghoul	scare	frighten
bat	~~goblin~~	scream	ghost
black cat	haunted	shout	orange
blood	horror	spider	pumpkin
boo	jack o lantern	treat	vampire
costume	night	trick	web
			witch

Mixed-up Mystery Words

A. Unscramble   B. Match

1. tab

— — —

2. wol

— — —

3. hstgo

— — — — —

4. thiwc

— — — — —

5. munpipk

— — — — — — —

6. eeonsklt

— — — — — — — —

7. bklca atc

— — — — —   — — —

Turn the pumpkin into a jack o'lantern

       Seasonal Activities

1. Cut   2. Paste to lined paper.   3. Write

Shawn felt strange as she ate the witch's cookie. She ran to the mirror and saw...

There is a prize at the annual Witches' Convention for the perfect magic potion. What would you put in your cauldron? What would it do?

On Halloween night, I dressed up like a ghost and started down the street. Suddenly...

       Seasonal Activities

Complete the Haunted House

___ Color the house. Cut it out. Cut and fold the front door open.

___ Paste the house to the middle of a large sheet of white paper.

___ Add these to your picture:

- fence across the front yard
- a black cat on the roof
- big yellow moon
- black trees

- jack o'lanterns along the fence
- witch flying across the sky
- bats flying out of the chimney

- a skeleton inside the front door (then fold the door shut)
- ghosts and goblins peeking from the windows

___ Color in the sky to look like Halloween night.

                                                           Seasonal Activities

Finish the picture.

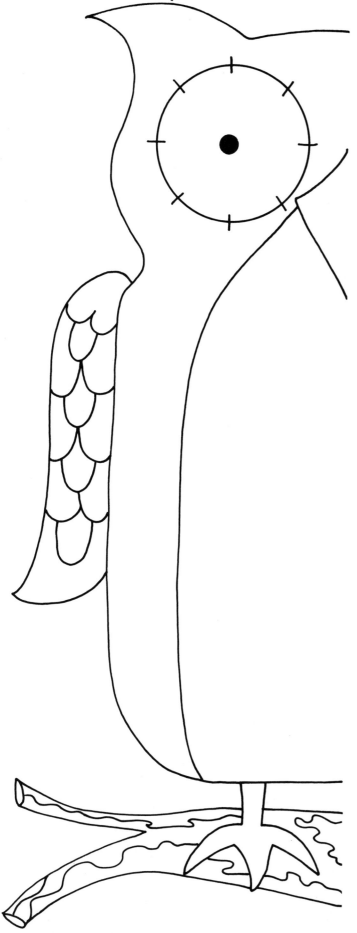

Circle each word in the puzzle as you find it.
You will find words across, down and diagonally.
A few words are written backwards.

Thanksgiving

```
A L E N G E D R F A W S T N V I A
M P T M B C A B P R R O S D R L W
C T H A N K S G I V I N G E J F R
S U K Y B D O P L S M E L S T R A
R R J F E A S T G H P C N O N O M
D K B L R U E O R I U P I D L M E
S E I O R T F T I B M N O W S T R
N Y T W I U E A M N E R T U M L I
U S A E E M U F A T D S H A G T C
D E E R S N S O A U E I S L K V A
C H R G H I D R K V T S A O L A M
H N O V E M B E R M S T U N C P U
I K M H V E O A Y S E C T E S T B
G N K E L U H W I L D E R N E S S
J S H E L P O Z M E T H A X T K R
O L C O W A I C L D Y N F I S H F
```

Cross out each word as you find it.

America	fish	November	wilderness
autumn	friends	nuts	Indians
berries	harvest	Pilgrim	Mayflower
celebrate	help	Thanksgiving	eat
deer	hunt	turkey	feast

Put this picture together to find out what the Pilgrim is doing.

Cut and paste.

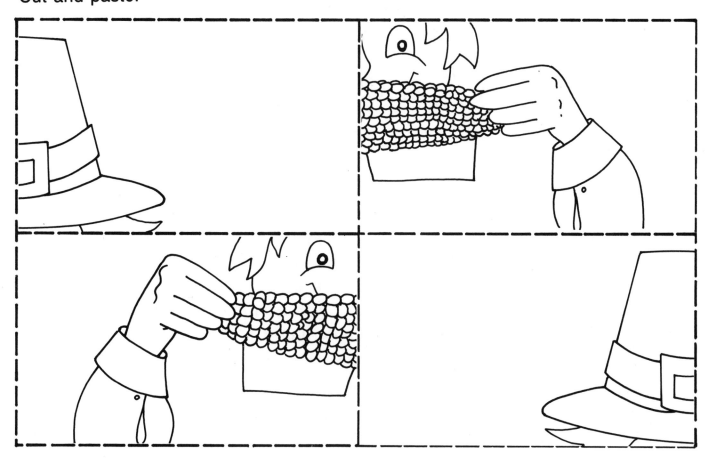

35

Pilgrims

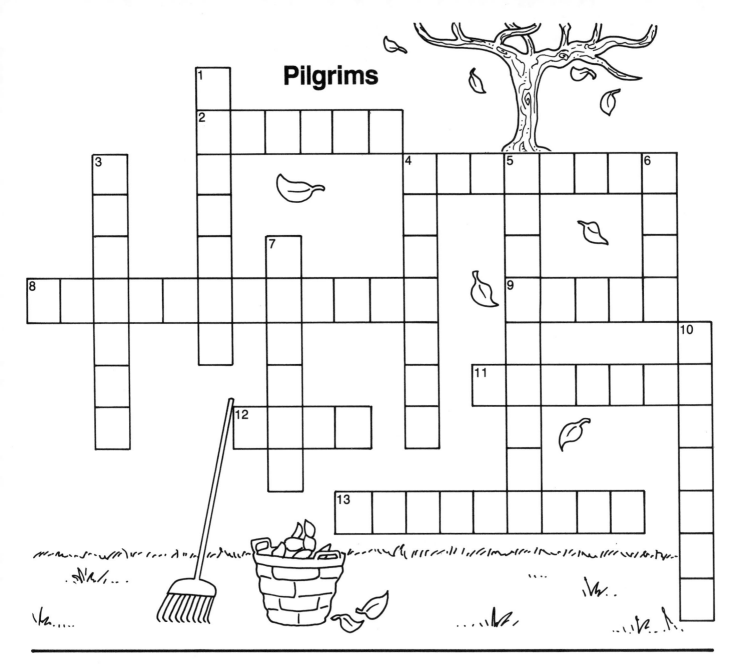

Across

2. another name for fall
4. _____ Rock
8. a holiday in November
9. a special meal
11. white, fluffy kernels you can eat
12. a forest animal used for food
13. to keep a holiday

Down

1. to gather the crops
3. an Indian friend of the Pilgrims
4. a person who came on the Mayflower
5. the Pilgrims' ship
6. to search for food
7. the season after autumn
10. the native Americans

Squanto	feast	autumn	deer	Plymouth
winter	Thanksgiving	Mayflower	popcorn	harvest
Indians	pilgrim	celebrate	hunt	

Seasonal Activities

THANKSGIVING WORDSEARCH

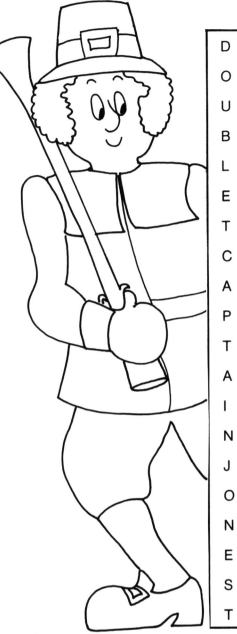

```
D I M A Y F L O W E R B P D P H N G H N
O L W A M P A N O A G I N D I A N S O C
U A P L Y M O U T H R O C K L R A P C E
B N A L O F T N T D C D O V G S T E W L
L T S A F U L E M E S F R O R H L E I E
E T S Z S A M O S E T B E Y I W A D L B
T R E N C H E R W R U R P A M I N W L R
C U N V J O U R N E Y E O G S N Y E I A
A N G A T H E R T T R E P E W T I L A T
P D E N G L A N D U X C C E O E C L M I
T L R F U T S R A R P H O A F R G L B O
A E S W M T J V V K I E R M P Q L S R N
I B F A R E S R S E H S N E P A M N A H
N E I D I K E L M Y S B R R F A R E D O
J D S L Q L S Q U A N T O I L O C B F R
O P H K E K O C E A N U S C C I U T O N
N X K V I J Y R J M A S S A S O I T R B
E L A I C P I Z S T O R M Y S E A S D O
S R H M I L E S S T A N D I S H G A Y O
T H U N T E R S C O M M O N H O U S E K
```

AMERICA	HARVEST	SAMOSET
BREECHES	HORNBOOK	SAILORS
CAPTAIN JONES	HUNTERS	SHIP
CELEBRATION	JOURNEY	SPEEDWELL
CLAMS	LOFT	SQUANTO
COMMON HOUSE	MASSASOIT	STEW
CORN	MAYFLOWER	STORMY SEAS
DEER	MAYFLOWER	TRAVELER
DOUBLET	COMPACT	TRENCHER
ENGLAND	MILES STANDISH	TRUNDLE BED
FALL	NUTS	TURKEY
FEAST	OCEANUS	VOYAGE
FISH	PASSENGERS	WAMPANOAG
GATHER	PILGRIMS	INDIANS
	PLYMOUTH ROCK	WILLIAM BRADFORD
	POPCORN	WINTER

The Mayflower

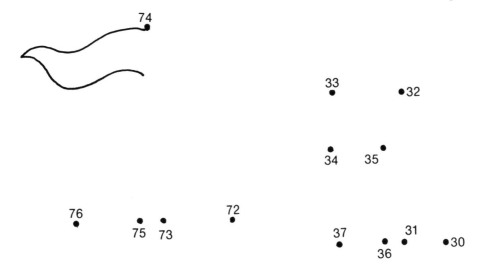

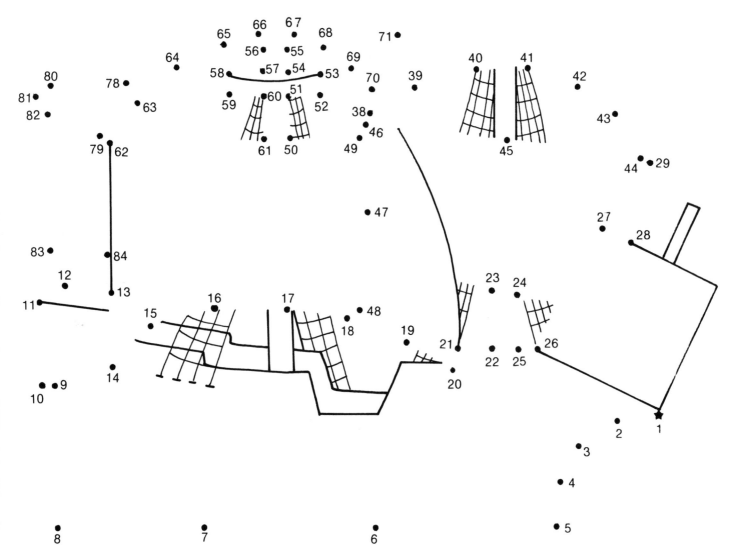

Seasonal Activities

All Aboard the Mayflower

1. Color the ship and background (p. 38).

2. Use the pattern below.
   Cut from brown construction paper to make the ship.
   Use the same pattern to cut several sheets of lined paper. Write your story about the Mayflower's journey. Use as many as you need.

brown ship

Mayflower

paper for story

3. Staple the story and brown ship to your large ship page.

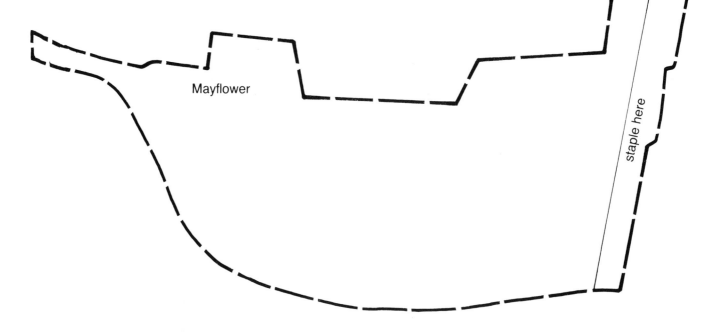

Mayflower

staple here

Draw the crew.

Are the Pilgrims on deck?

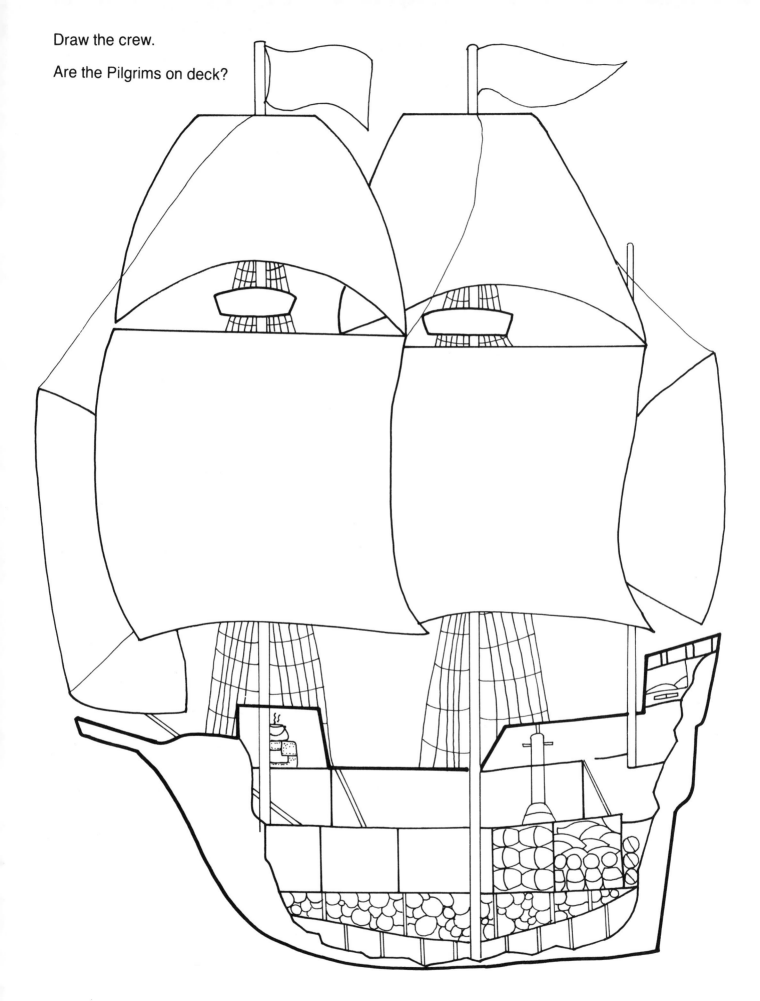

Seasonal Activities

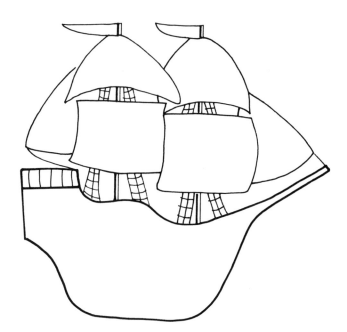

September

S	M	T	W	Th	F	S

The Mayflower Voyage

It began on _____

There were _____ passengers.

Name 3 interesting events
  that happened on the ship:

_____

_____

_____

_____

_____

They sighted land on _____

_____

October

S	M	T	W	Th	F	S

November

S	M	T	W	Th	F	S

My name is _____

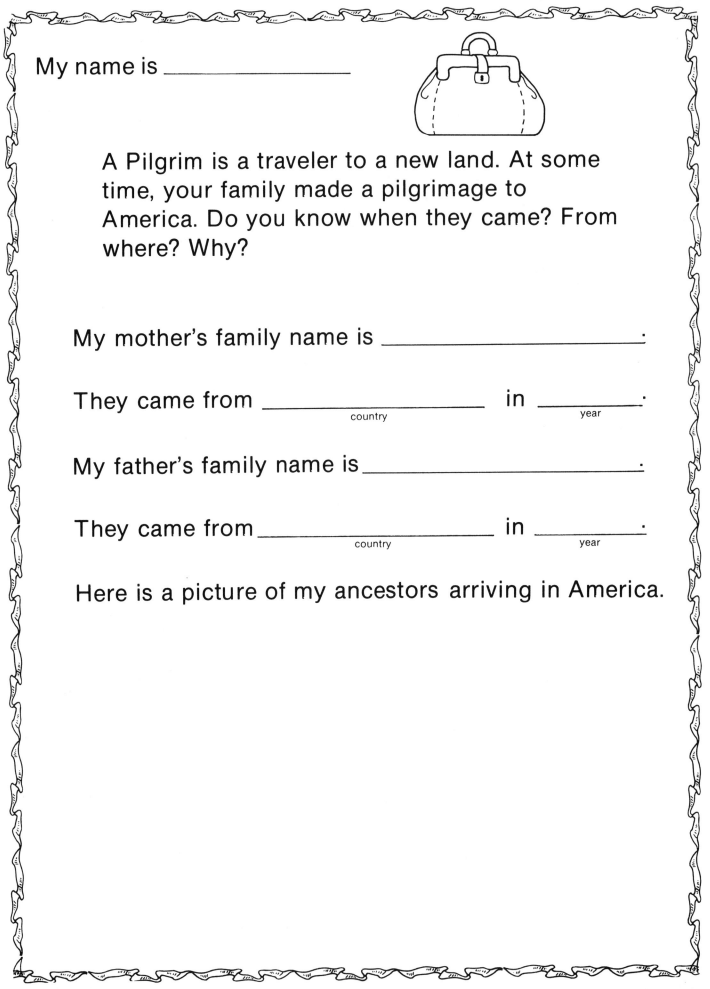

A Pilgrim is a traveler to a new land. At some time, your family made a pilgrimage to America. Do you know when they came? From where? Why?

My mother's family name is _____ .

They came from _____ in _____ .
country   year

My father's family name is _____ .

They came from _____ in _____ .
country   year

Here is a picture of my ancestors arriving in America.

Seasonal Activities

The Pilgrims traveled across a vast sea to get to a strange land to start a new life.

Imagine that you are a "pilgrim" traveling through space to start a new life on a strange planet.

I. Describe your ship and what happens on your journey.

II. Describe the planet and how you would start your new home.

III. Illustrate your new home.

Seasonal Activities

1. Cut out a story starter   2. Paste to lined paper   3. Write

One fall day in 1620, a pilgrim boy was walking through the woods. Suddenly, he was face to face with an Indian boy...

I really love to eat — especially at big family dinners! Let me tell you about the perfect Thanksgiving feast...

Sailing on the Mayflower sure isn't easy. Here's what it is *really* like...

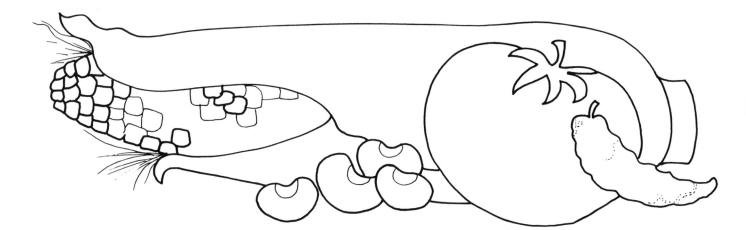

New World Food Plants

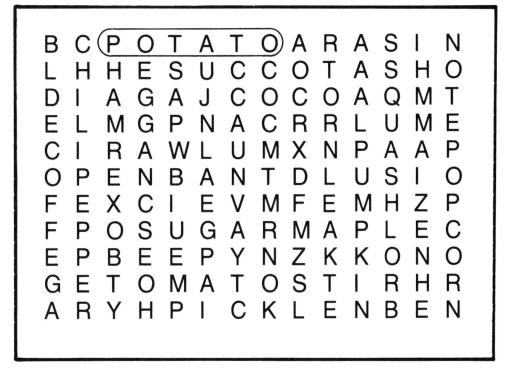

```
B  C (P  O  T  A  T  O) A  R  A  S  I  N
L  H  H  E  S  U  C  C  O  T  A  S  H  O
D  I  A  G  A  J  C  O  C  O  A  Q  M  T
E  L  M  G  P  N  A  C  R  R  L  U  M  E
C  I  R  A  W  L  U  M  X  N  P  A  A  P
O  P  E  N  B  A  N  T  D  L  U  S  I  O
F  E  X  C  I  E  V  M  F  E  M  H  Z  P
F  P  O  S  U  G  A  R  M  A  P  L  E  C
E  P  B  E  E  P  Y  N  Z  K  K  O  N  O
G  E  T  O  M  A  T  O  S  T  I  R  H  R
A  R  Y  H  P  I  C  K  L  E  N  B  E  N
```

✓ potato	___ corn
___ succotash	___ sugar maple
___ pumpkin	___ cocoa
___ peanut	___ chili pepper
___ squash	___ lima beans
___ tomato	___ maize
___ popcorn	

One Word (title)	
Two Words (describe title)	
Three Words (action)	
Four Words (feeling)	
One Word (refer back to title)	

Turkey Cinquain

Seasonal Activities

Thanksgiving Pie

Ask 20 people to describe their favorite pie.
Record it on this graph.

	pumpkin	apple	lemon	banana cream	mince	other
15						
14						
13						
12						
11						
10						
9						
8						
7						
6						
5						
4						
3						
2						
1						

Which pie did most people choose? _____

Seasonal Activities

Thanksgiving Dinner

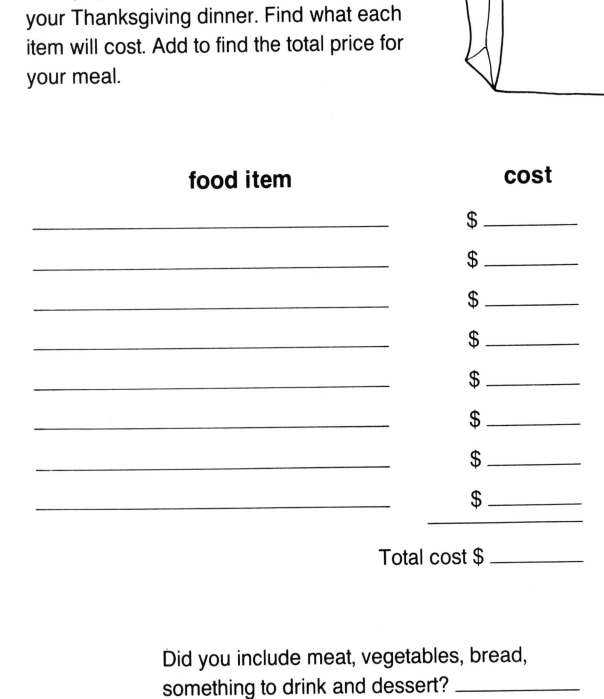

You will need the grocery store ads from a newspaper. Select the foods you want for your Thanksgiving dinner. Find what each item will cost. Add to find the total price for your meal.

food item	cost
_____	$ _____
_____	$ _____
_____	$ _____
_____	$ _____
_____	$ _____
_____	$ _____
_____	$ _____
_____	$ _____

Total cost $ _____

Did you include meat, vegetables, bread, something to drink and dessert? _____

Thanksgiving Jigsaw

Seasonal Activities

Use the code to answer the riddles.

A–1	G–7	M–13	P–16	T–20
C–3	I–9	N–14	R–18	Y–25
E–5	L–12	O–15	S–19	

1. First I'm yellow and hard. Add heat.
   Now I'm white and soft. What am I?

   16   15   16   3   15   18   14

   __ __ __ __ __ __ __

2. If April showers bring May flowers, what do Mayflowers bring?

   16   9   12   7   18   9   13   19

   __ __ __ __ __ __ __ __

3. Why can't you tell a secret in a cornfield?

   20 15 15   13 1 14 25   5 1 18 19

   __ __ __   __ __ __ __   __ __ __ __

   1 18 5   12 9 19 20 5 14 9 14 7

   __ __ __   __ __ __ __ __ __ __ __ __

Seasonal Activities

Winter Activities

Name It!

❄	an animal	something to eat	a country	something to wear	a girl's name
example **A**	anteater	artichoke	Australia	anklets	Anna
W					
I					
N					
T					
E					
R					

December	year	The season is: winter summer spring fall

Sunday	Monday	Tuesday	Wednesday	Thursday	Friday	Saturday

1. Write the number for each day in December.
2. There are always _____ days in December.
3. Draw a snowman on the first day of winter.
4. Draw a green wreath around Christmas Day.
5. Color each day of winter vacation.
6. Record class birthdays on your calendar.

Turn this page over and show one way your family celebrates Christmas or Hanukkah.

January	year	The season is: winter summer spring fall

Sunday	Monday	Tuesday	Wednesday	Thursday	Friday	Saturday

1. Write the number for each day in January.
2. There are always _____ days in January.
3. Make a big star on New Year's Day.
4. Outline the date of Martin Luther King, Jr.'s birthday.
5. What day of the week is January 16th? _____
6. Record class birthdays on your calendar.

Turn this paper over and show your favorite winter activity.

        Seasonal Activities

February	year	The season is: winter summer spring fall

Sunday	Monday	Tuesday	Wednesday	Thursday	Friday	Saturday

1. Write the number for each day in February.
2. There are usually _____ days in February.
   In leap years there are _____ days.
3. Color Groundhog's Day black like a shadow.
4. Draw a red heart on Valentine's Day.
5. Circle the birthdays of George Washington
   and Abraham Lincoln.
6. Record class birthdays on your calendar.

Turn this paper over and draw you and your shadow.

Winter Holidays

Holidays representing many cultures and religions occur during the winter months. You might select several that share a common theme or select those you feel are important for your students to know about. Plan activities that are appropriate to the age and ability of your students. Look for the elements of sharing and caring that occur in these celebrations.

For example:
- Christmas (Christian countries and cultures)
- Winter Solstice (Many Native American tribes)
- Kwanzaa (Afro-Americans)
- Hanukkah (Jews)

Think About It

Does everyone in America celebrate Christmas?

Do you or someone you know celebrate a different holiday?

Is one celebration better than another? Why or why not?

Do these different holidays have anything in common?

How do we learn about what holidays mean and how to celebrate them?

Many times gifts are given at celebrations. Why does this happen?

Can you think of a "gift" you can give that would be very special but is not something that can be wrapped in paper and ribbon?

How do you think Santa Claus became a part of Christmas?

56

Christmas

One of the most important days in the Christian year is Christmas, the day set aside to celebrate the birth of Jesus. Share the story of the journey to Bethlehem, his birth in the stable, of the star guiding the Wise Men. Discuss how, while it is a religious holiday for Christians, Christmas has become a time of gift-giving and feasts for many other people also.

Read books about the Christmas season.

> *Holly, Reindeer, and Colored Lights* by Edna Barth; Houghton, 1971
> *The Family Christmas Tree Book* by Tomie de Paola; Holiday, 1980
> *The Fir Tree* by Hans Christian Andersen; Harper, 1970
> *The Cobweb Christmas* by Shirley Climo; Harper, 1982
> *The Clown of God* by Tomie de Paola; Harcourt, 1978
> *Nine Days to Christmas* by Marie Ets & Aurora Labastida; Viking, 1959
> *Mousekin's Christmas Eve* by Edna Miller; Prentice, 1965
> *Pedro, the Angel of Olivera Street* by Leo Politi; Scribners, 1946
> *It's Christmas* by Jack Prelutsky; Greenwillow, 1981
> *The Best Christmas Pageant Ever* by Barbara Robinson; Avon, 1972
> *The Twelve Days of Christmas* by Jan Brett; Putnam, 1986
> *Carl's Christmas* by Alexandra Day; Farrar, Straus, Giroux, 1990

Explore how Christmas is celebrated in other countries. For example:

Santa Lucia — Sweden
Early on Santa Lucia's day, the oldest girl in the family, wearing a white robe and a crown of candles, brings coffee and saffron buns to the adults.

Los Posadas — Mexico
For eight nights before Christmas, people re-enact the search of Mary and Joseph for shelter. They go to a home and ask to be let in. The owner of the home refuses at first, then invites them in for a party.

Polish Celebrations
Celebrating begins on Christmas Eve and lasts until January 6th. Straw under the table represents the manger. An empty place is left at the table for any stranger coming to the house. The oldest person at the table takes a bite from a rice wafer symbolizing love of peace. The wafer passes from person to person ending with the youngest child.

Have children who do celebrate Christmas explain what occurs in their family.

Kwanzaa

Kwanzaa is an Afro-American holiday. For seven days activities are organized around seven principles (unity, self-determination, collective work and responsibility, cooperative economics, purpose, creativity, and faith). Each day one of the seven principles is explored and a candle is lit for the principle.

Create murals about Black life in the past and today.
Share poetry and music by Black artists.

Discuss (to the ability of your students) what each of the principles mean.

Have children design banners in red, black, and green.
red — struggle, black — for Afro-Americans, green — for children (the hope of the future)

Have children in your class who celebrate Kwanzaa explain what their families do.

Let's Celebrate Kwanzaa by Helen Davis Thompson; Gumbs and Thomas Publishers, 1989
The Kwanzaa Coloring Book by Balerie J. R. Banks; Sala Enterprises, 1985 (contains information, maps, activities...not just a coloring book)

Hanukkah

Hanukkah is one of many Jewish religious holidays. It honors an ancient struggle against the Syrians who occupied Jerusalem and tried to force the Jews to worship other gods. When the Jews drove the invaders away, they found only enough oil in the temple lamp for one day. Miraculously it lasted for eight days, giving them renewed courage. They celebrate today by lighting candles for eight nights.

Share books about Hannukah with your students.

Hanukkah Money by Sholom Aleichem; Greenwillow, 1978
A Picture Book of Hanukkah by David Adler; Holiday, 1982
The Hanukkah Story by Marilyn Hirsh; Hebrew, 1977
I Love Hanukkah by Marilyn Hirsh; Holiday, 1984
Laughing Latkes by Marilyn Goffstein; Farrar, 1981
Hanukkah, The Festival of Lights by Jenny Koralek; Lothrop, Lee & Shepard, 1987
The Chanukkah Guest by Eric A. Kimmel, Holiday House, 1990

Have a menorah in class and explain how the holiday is celebrated. Make a menorah (paint, paper, clay) and write about its significance on Hanukkah.

Teach the children how to play the dreidel game.

Have children who celebrate Hanukkah explain what their family does.

Writing Activities for Winter Holidays

- Interview a friend and write about his/her holiday memory.

  _____ at My House
  (holiday name)

  _____ When I Was a Child
  (holiday name)

- Write about your own memories:

  My Earliest _____ Memory
  (holiday name)

  The Best Part of _____
  (holiday name)

- Christmas

  Write about the first Christmas:
  The Wise Men

  Mary and Joseph

  The Gifts of the Magi

  Write about Santa Claus:
  Santa's elves are very upset. A terrible disaster has happened in the toy factory.

  Christmas Eve is over. Now Santa Claus will...

  Mrs. Claus has been busy all year. It is her responsibility to...

- Kwanzaa

  The Principle of _____
  (Write about the one you feel is the most important)

  Red, Black, and Green—Symbols of Kwanzaa

  A Family Celebration

  Kwanzaa is almost here and there are no candles to be had. What can we do?

- Hanukkah

  Re-tell the story of the first Hanukkah celebration in the temple after the Syrians had been defeated.

  The Miracle of the Oil

  Grandfather's Menorah

  My First Memory of Hanukkah

  The Best Part of Hanukkah

December

Christmas	Hanukkah	Winter

1. Read   2. Cut   3. Paste

Br-r-r!	light Menorah candles	Santa comes the 25th.
decorate the tree	wear mittens and earmuffs	time for ice skating
hang your stocking	Yum! Potato pancakes.	surprises under the tree
Children play with dreidels.	build a snowman	The Feast of Lights

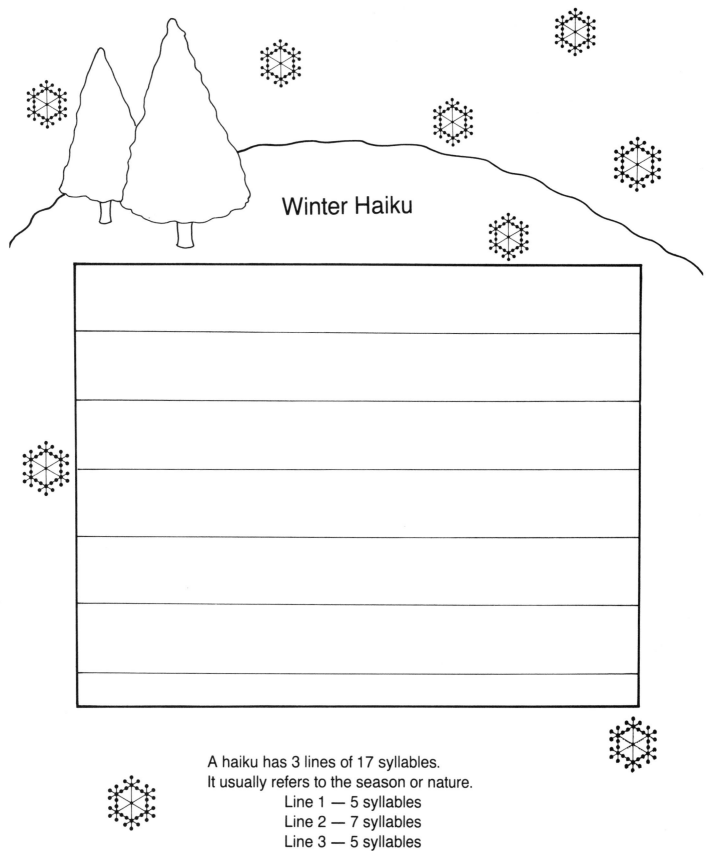

Winter Haiku

A haiku has 3 lines of 17 syllables.
It usually refers to the season or nature.

Line 1 — 5 syllables
Line 2 — 7 syllables
Line 3 — 5 syllables

Start with the thought, then adjust the syllables.

Which words go together?

kid

kitten

joey

lamb

gosling

cub

tadpole

puppy

caterpillar

child

duckling

calf

chick

foal

Word Box

frog	adult	cow
chicken	kangaroo	dog
goat	goose	duck
cat	sheep	butterfly
bear	horse	

Seasonal Activities

1. Draw   3. Paste to lined paper

2. Cut   4. Write a story.

Seasonal Activities

Christmas

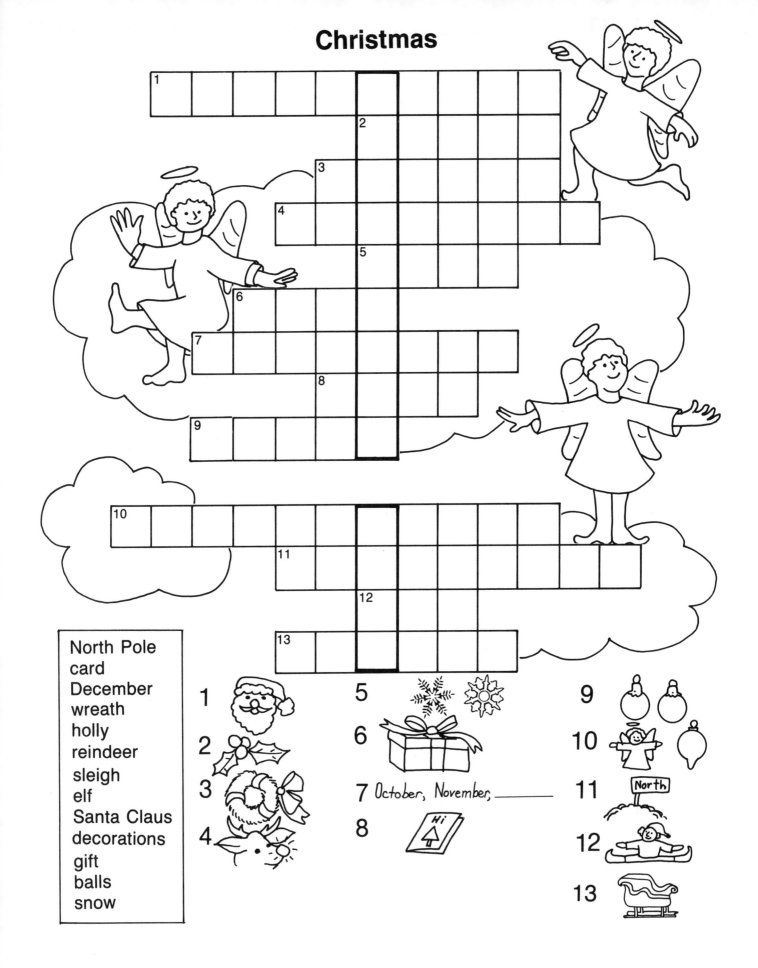

North Pole
card
December
wreath
holly
reindeer
sleigh
elf
Santa Claus
decorations
gift
balls
snow

1

2

3

4

5

6

7 October, November, _____

8

9

10

11

12

13

Draw the secret word on the back of this paper.

Seasonal Activities

The First Christmas

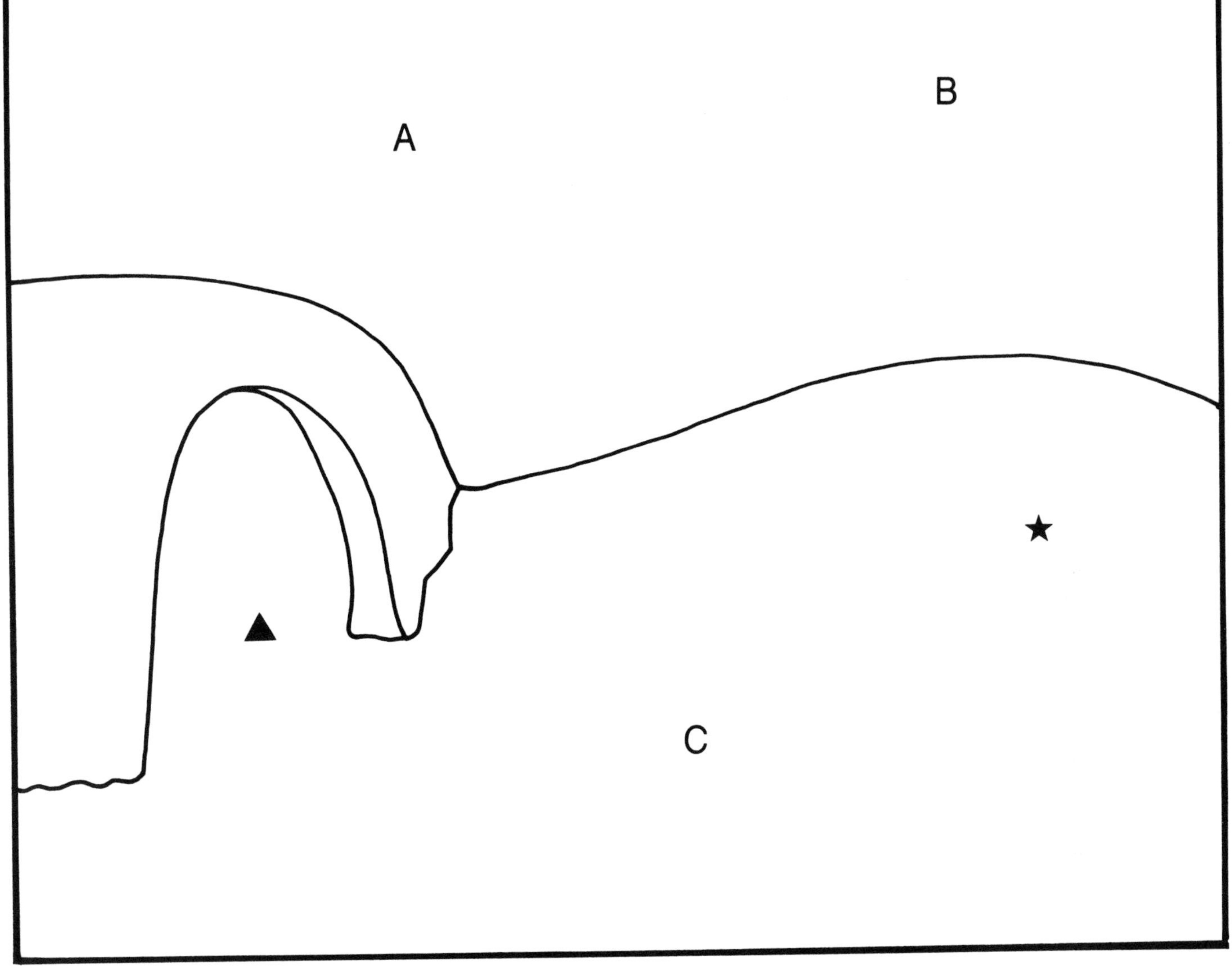

A

B

★

▲

C

1. Color   2. Cut   3. Paste

Paste on A.

Paste on ▲.

Paste on C.

Paste on B.

Paste on ★.

Drawing Fun

Who is pulling Santa's sleigh?
Follow the steps and draw the surprise in the box.

1. Follow the drawing steps.

2. Color the reindeer brown. His antlers are black.

3. Add yellow sleigh bells on a red ribbon.

         Seasonal Activities

Plurals

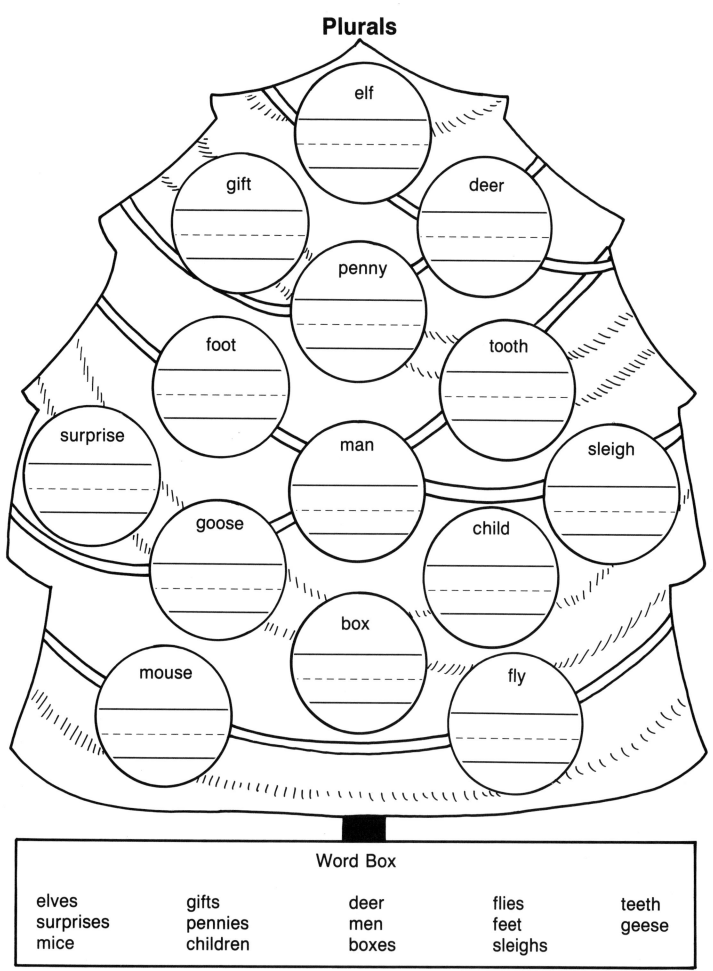

elf

gift

deer

penny

foot

tooth

surprise

man

sleigh

goose

child

mouse

box

fly

Word Box

elves	gifts	deer	flies	teeth
surprises	pennies	men	feet	geese
mice	children	boxes	sleighs	

Seasonal Activities

Note: Run this pattern on construction paper.

What's In Santa's Pack?

fold

1. Color.
2. Cut - - - and fold _____.
3. Open. Write or draw what you could find in Santa's pack.

Seasonal Activities

Riddle Time

Write your Christmas riddle on the outside.
Write and draw the answer inside.

fold

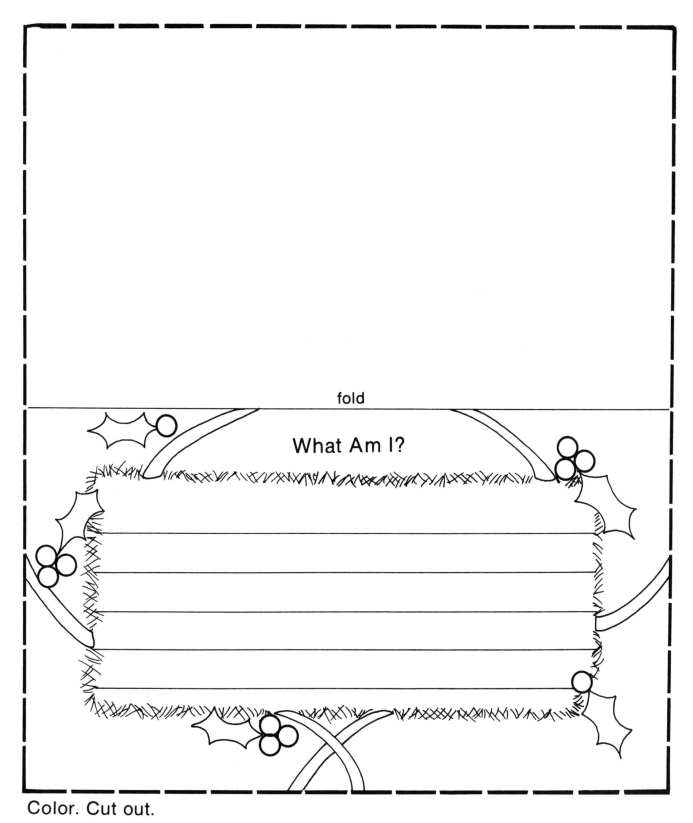

What Am I?

Color. Cut out.

Seasonal Activities

Connect the dots.

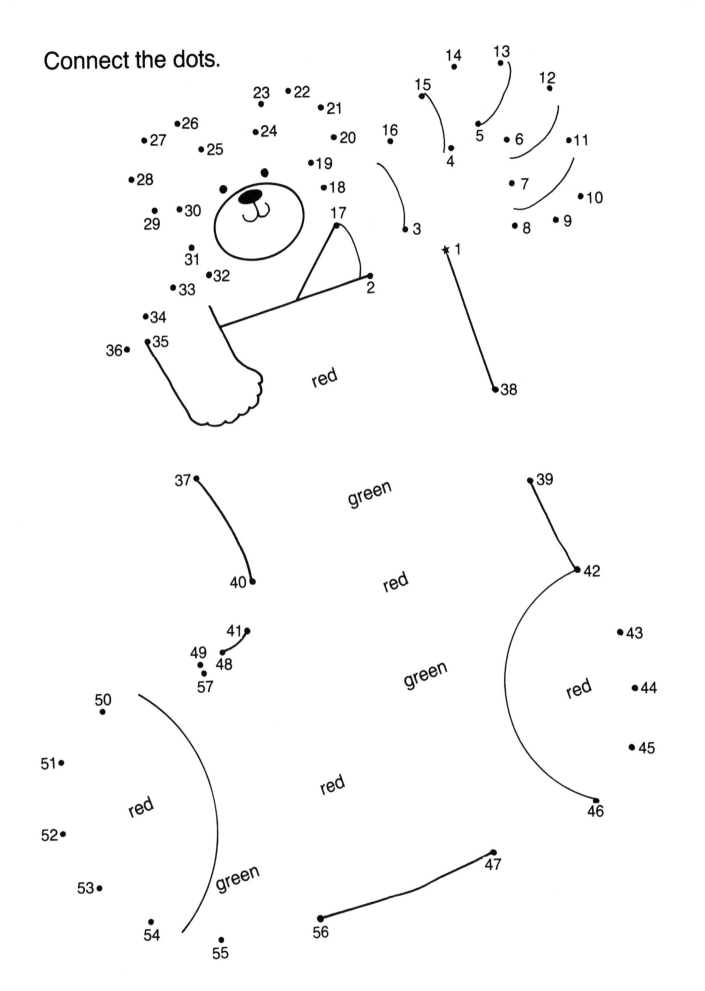

red

green

red

green

red

red

red

green

Deck the Halls...

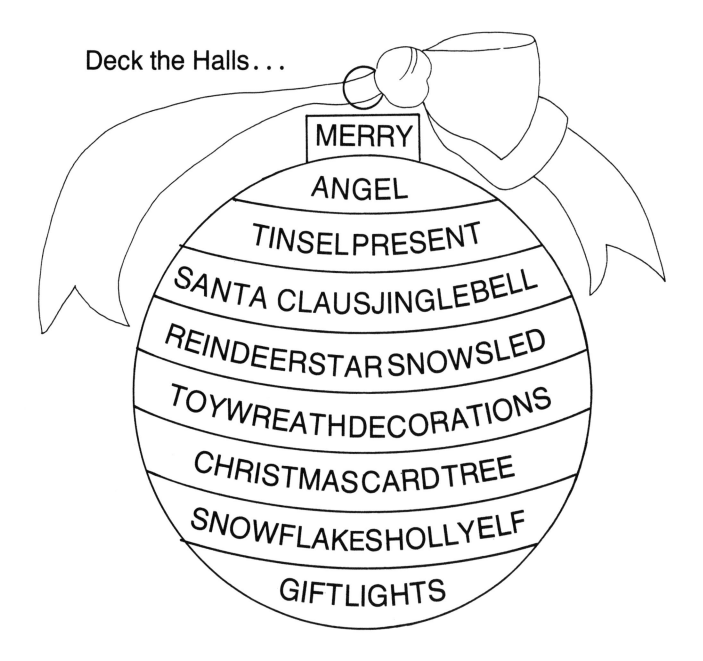

MERRY
ANGEL
TINSELPRESENT
SANTA CLAUSJINGLEBELL
REINDEERSTARSNOWSLED
TOYWREATHDECORATIONS
CHRISTMASCARDTREE
SNOWFLAKESHOLLYELF
GIFTLIGHTS

Circle and Color these words:

yellow	green	red	
MERRY	DECORATIONS	ANGEL	REINDEER
	GIFT	BELL	SANTA CLAUS
	LIGHTS	CARD	SLED
	PRESENT	CHRISTMAS	SNOW
	TINSEL	ELF	SNOWFLAKES
	TOY	HOLLY	STAR
	WREATH	JINGLE	TREE

Unscramble these Christmas Words:

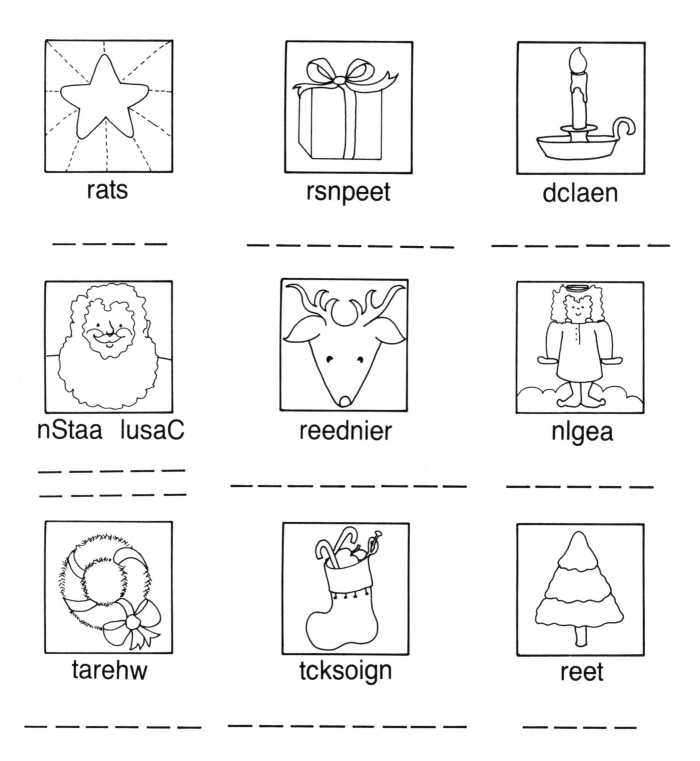

rats

rsnpeet

dclaen

‐ ‐ ‐ ‐

‐ ‐ ‐ ‐ ‐ ‐ ‐

‐ ‐ ‐ ‐ ‐ ‐

nStaa lusaC

reednier

nlgea

‐ ‐ ‐ ‐ ‐

‐ ‐ ‐ ‐ ‐

tarehw

tcksoign

reet

‐ ‐ ‐ ‐ ‐ ‐

‐ ‐ ‐ ‐ ‐ ‐ ‐ ‐

‐ ‐ ‐ ‐

angel	star	present
candle	wreath	reindeer
tree	stocking	Santa Claus

Silent Night, Christmas Night

```
R  E  I  N  D  E  E  R  C  E  L  E  B  R  A  T  E
S  W  G  I  F  T  Y  S  A  N  T  A  C  L  A  U  S
T  R  S  I  S  E  N  N  F  R  X  N  A  B  O  H  I
A  E  D  L  N  T  M  O  I  E  L  G  R  M  P  P  L
R  A  T  M  E  G  O  W  R  L  B  E  D  L  A  O  E
E  T  I  R  C  I  E  C  P  T  N  L  O  O  C  I  N
K  H  N  H  E  Q  G  R  K  K  H  D  P  V  K  N  T
C  F  S  Y  C  E  G  H  B  I  U  P  J  E  A  S  N
P  R  E  S  E  N  T  V  O  R  N  A  O  N  G  E  I
E  G  L  I  G  H  T  S  T  S  E  G  S  L  E  T  G
P  A  C  K  C  H  R  I  S  T  M  A  S  R  E  T  H
F  E  A  S  T  O  I  J  W  F  O  O  D  T  Q  I  T
H  C  A  N  D  L  E  S  L  L  A  M  B  B  U  A  Z
C  O  O  K  Y  L  D  E  C  O  R  A  T  I  O  N  S
S  H  A  R  E  Y  M  I  S  T  L  E  T  O  E  Y  A
J  I  N  G  L  E  B  E  L  L  S  C  R  E  C  H  E
```

ANGEL	FOOD	POINSETTA
CANDLES	GIFT	REINDEER
CARD	GINGERBREAD BOY	RUDOLPH
CELEBRATE	HOLLY	SANTA CLAUS
CHIMNEY	JINGLE BELLS	SHARE
CHRISTMAS	LAMB	SILENT NIGHT
COOKY	LIGHTS	SLEIGH
CRECHE	LOVE	SNOW
DECORATIONS	MISTLETOE	STAR
ELF	NORTH POLE	STOCKING
FIR	PACK	TINSEL
FEAST	PACKAGE	TREE
	PRESENT	WREATH

Once upon a Christmas Time

Write a paragraph describing a favorite Christmas memory. Then illustrate your paragraph.

Here are some ideas to help you get started.

☐ Your Own Memories

1. My Earliest Christmas Memory
2. The Best Part of Christmas
3. My favorite Christmas Gift

☐ A Friend's Christmas Memory
Interview a friend or relative, then write.

1. _____'s Favorite Christmas
   name
2. Christmas When I Was A Child
3. Christmas in _____
   country

☐ The First Christmas
Re-tell the story of the first Christmas experience from the point of view of:

1. The Wise Men
2. Mary and Joseph
3. A Poor Shepherd Boy

       Seasonal Activities

Stocking Surprises

1. Place this page on a sheet of lined paper.
2. Cut out the stocking and the lined paper at the same time.
3. Write about what you would like to find in your Christmas stocking.
4. Glue your story and stocking together at the top.

Seasonal Activities

Follow the directions below to finish this picture.

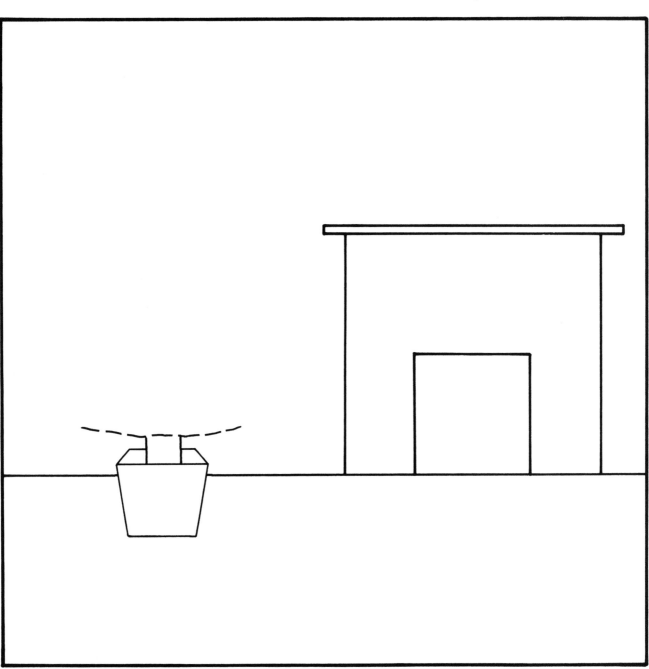

___Draw a large, green Christmas tree in the blue box.

___Put these ornaments on the tree:
  ___ a large yellow star on top
  ___ 9 colorful balls
  ___ 5 red and white candy canes
  ___ a long string of lights

___Make five beautiful presents under the tree.

___Make the fireplace look like reddish-brown brick.

___Draw three stockings hanging on the fireplace.
Make each one different.

___Put a large wreath with a big red bow over the fireplace

___Make a kitten sleeping on a rug in front of the fireplace.

1. Choose a story beginning.   2. Paste it to a sheet of paper.   3. Write

Santa's elves are very upset. A terrible disaster has happened in the toy factory.

Christmas Eve is over. Now Santa Claus will...

Getting presents is always fun, but to me the best part of Christmas is...

Mrs. Claus has been busy all year. It is her responsibility to...

        Seasonal Activities

Color the boxes to find the mystery picture.

1	milk	tomato	pepper	pie	jellybean	bread	fish	cake	chicken
2	cloud	rain	thunder	pencil	teddy bear	chalk	wind	snow	sunshine
3	cap	scarf	glove	sock	boot	slipper	dress	shirt	belt
4	toes	knee	nose	sled	chin	eye	lips	finger	arm
5	chair	table	plane	bird	blimp	marble	jet	bed	stool
6	cabbage	banana	lime	grape	pineapple	apple	pear	peach	spinach
7	barn	rose	ball	tulip	daisy	daffodil	jumprope	geranium	shed
8	red	top	yellow	blue	doll	purple	orange	kite	brown
9	Jo Ellen	Anna	Bill	Marilyn	Lucy	Olive	Earl	Ginny	Joy
10	Texas	New York	Idaho	Oregon	tractor	Iowa	Ohio	Utah	Nevada
11	under	over	into	above	fir tree	below	next	after	by
12	elf	fairy	pixie	juice	milk	lemonade	giant	unicorn	ghost

Row 1– Make all candy green.
Row 2– Color all things you can draw with green.
Row 3– Make everything you put on your feet green.
Row 4– Color everything on your face green.
Row 5– Make things that fly green.
Row 6– Make all fruit green.
Row 7– Color all flowers green.
Row 8– Make all color words green.
Row 9– Color all names green.
Row 10– Color all machines brown.
Row 11– Color plants brown.
Row 12– Color things you drink blue.
★ Color all toys on this page red.

Use the code to find the answers.

a-1	e-4	k-7	r-10	u-13
c-2	h-5	n-8	s-11	y-15
d-3	i-6	o-9	t-12	z-16

Where do gingerbread men sleep?

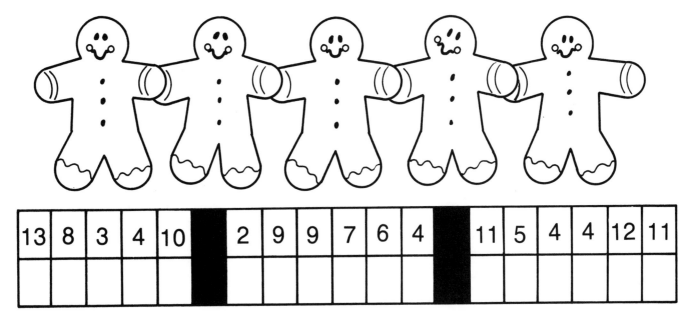

13	8	3	4	10	■	2	9	9	7	6	4	■	11	5	4	4	12	11
					■							■						

Why does Rudolph need an umbrella?

5	4	11	■	1
		,	■	

10	4	6	8	3	4	4	10

Seasonal Activities

A Recipe For the Perfect Christmas

Think about it:

What ingredients make Christmas special for your family?
people	activities	food
places	decorations	memories
_____	_____	_____

How do these mix together to make Christmas into a wonderful day?

Now...write your "recipe."

_____'s Recipe for a Perfect Christmas

Ingredients:

_____   _____
_____   _____
_____   _____
_____   _____

Directions:

_____
_____
_____
_____
_____
_____
_____
_____
_____
_____
_____

Start at ★.

Count by 2s.

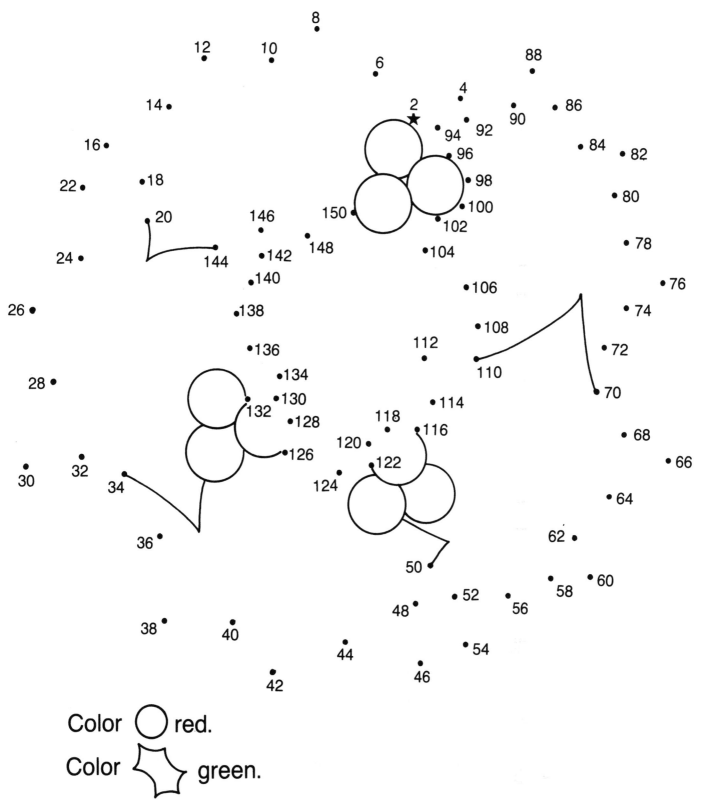

Color ◯ red.

Color ✦ green.

Gingerbread House

1. Color   2. Cut   3. Fold   4. Paste

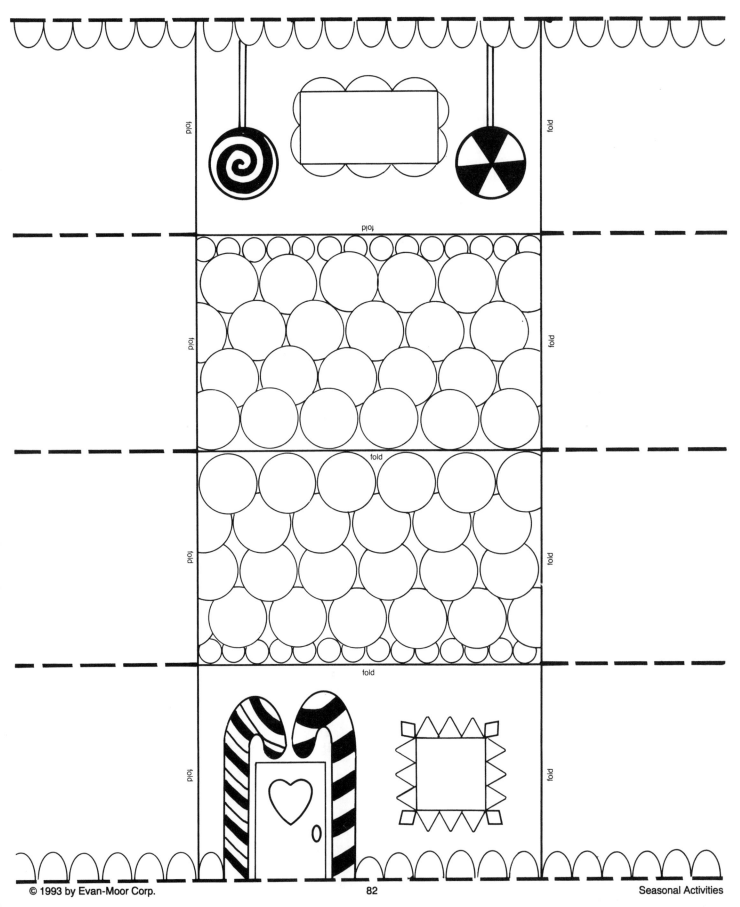

82   Seasonal Activities

The Months of the Year

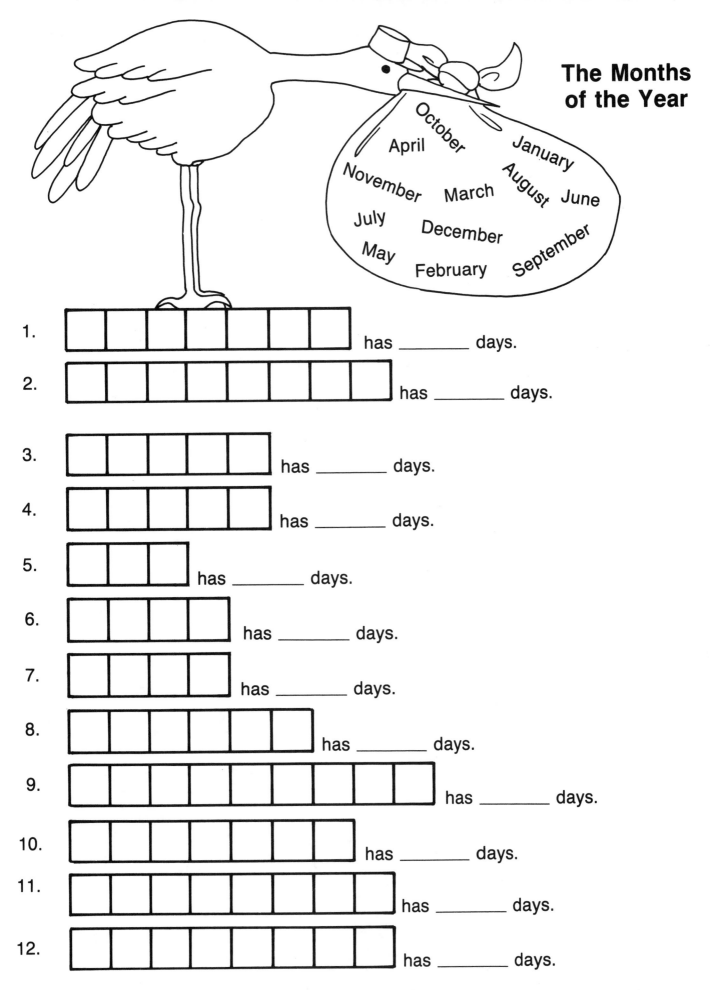

October April January November March August June July December September May February

1. ☐☐☐☐☐☐☐ has _____ days.

2. ☐☐☐☐☐☐☐☐ has _____ days.

3. ☐☐☐☐☐ has _____ days.

4. ☐☐☐☐☐ has _____ days.

5. ☐☐☐ has _____ days.

6. ☐☐☐☐ has _____ days.

7. ☐☐☐☐ has _____ days.

8. ☐☐☐☐☐☐ has _____ days.

9. ☐☐☐☐☐☐☐☐ has _____ days.

10. ☐☐☐☐☐☐☐ has _____ days.

11. ☐☐☐☐☐☐☐☐ has _____ days.

12. ☐☐☐☐☐☐☐☐ has _____ days.

Seasonal Activities

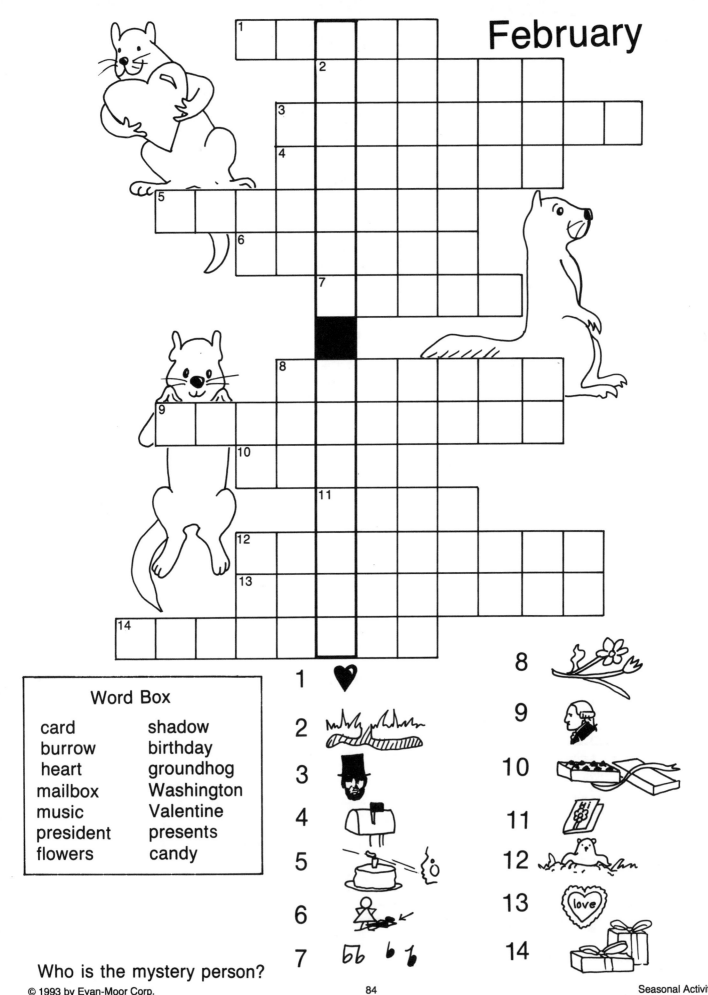

February

Word Box

card   shadow
burrow   birthday
heart   groundhog
mailbox   Washington
music   Valentine
president   presents
flowers   candy

1. ♥
2.
3.
4.
5.
6.
7.
8.
9.
10.
11.
12.
13.
14.

Who is the mystery person?

Seasonal Activities

You will find words across, down and diagonally.
A few words are written backwards.

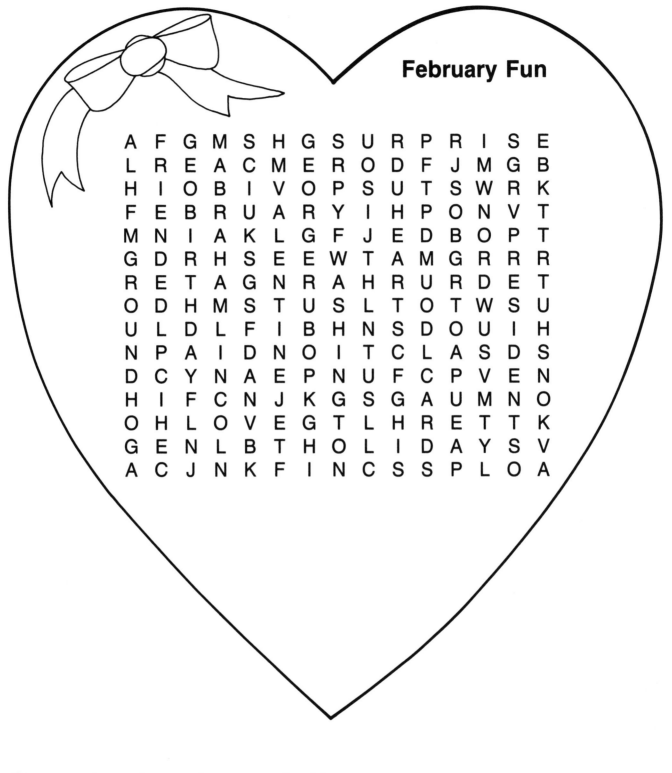

February Fun

```
A F G M S H G S U R P R I S E
L R E A C M E R O D F J M G B
H I O B I V O P S U T S W R K
F E B R U A R Y I H P O N V T
M N I A K L G F J E D B O P T
G D R H S E E W T A M G R R R
R E T A G N R A H R U R D E T
O D H M S T U S L T O T W S U
U L D L F I B H N S D O U I H
N P A I D N O I T C L A S D S
D C Y N A E P N U F C P V E N
H I F C N J K G S G A U M N O
O H L O V E G T L H R E T T K
G E N L B T H O L I D A Y S V
A C J N K F I N C S S P L O A
```

Cross out each word as you find it.

Abraham   February   George   holidays   presidents
birthday   friend   groundhog   Lincoln   shadow
cards   flower   heart   love   surprise
valentine   Washington

                                               Seasonal Activities

Groundhog Day

Paste the pictures in the correct place to complete the picture.

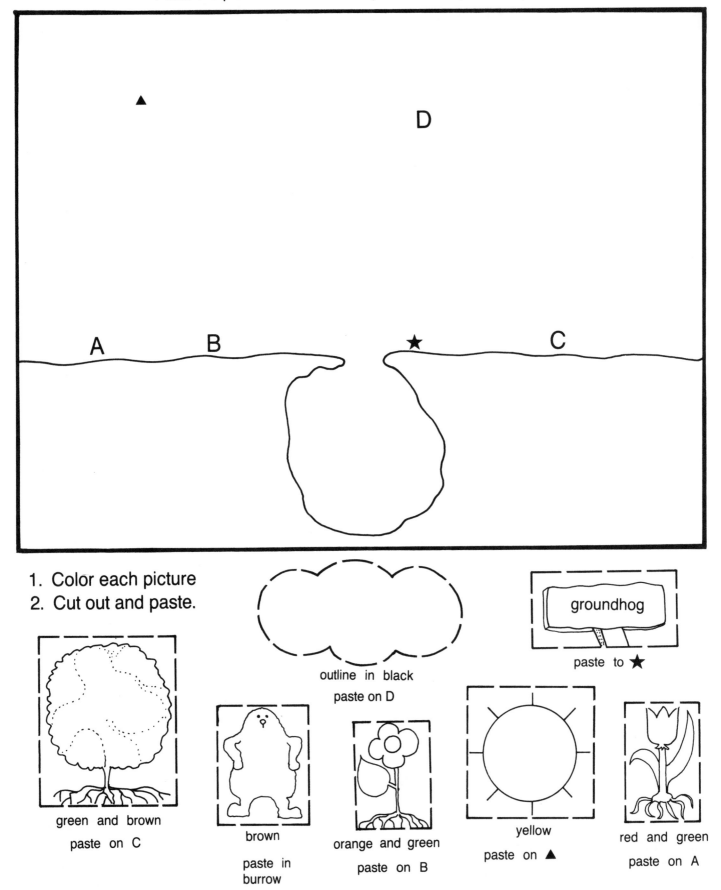

A   B   ★   C

D

1. Color each picture
2. Cut out and paste.

outline in black
paste on D

groundhog
paste to ★

green and brown
paste on C

brown
paste in
burrow

orange and green
paste on B

yellow
paste on ▲

red and green
paste on A

                   Seasonal Activities

Words that Describe

Weather Watch	Feelings
List the words that describe weather:	List emotion words here:
_____ _____	_____ _____
_____ _____	_____ _____
_____ _____	_____ _____
_____ _____	_____ _____
_____ _____	_____ _____
_____ _____	_____ _____
_____ _____	_____ _____
_____ _____	_____ _____
_____ _____	_____ _____
_____ _____	_____ _____

afraid	fainthearted	pleasant
alarmed	foggy	rainy
apprehensive	foul	shy
balmy	frightened	skittish
breezy	gusty	stormy
bright	hazy	sunshiny
brisk	inclement	terrified
cautious	jumpy	timid
cloudy	nervous	uneasy
cloudless	overcast	upset
dismayed	panicky	wary
		windy

Add one word of your own to each list.

Seasonal Activities

Contractions

can't

couldn't

didn't

doesn't

let's

aren't

you're

they're

he'll

I'm

isn't

won't

it's

Seasonal Activities

Valentine Messages

Use the code to solve the riddles.

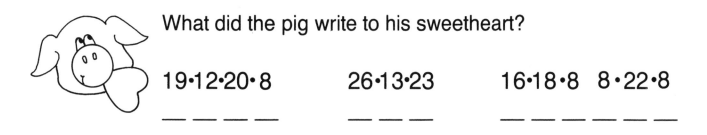

A–26	F–21	L–15	Q–10	V–5
B–25	G–20	M–14	R–9	W–4
C–24	H–19	N–13	S–8	X–3
D–23	I–18	O–12	T–7	Y–2
E–22	J–17	P–11	U–6	Z–1
	K–16			

What did the pig write to his sweetheart?

19·12·20·8   26·13·23   16·18·8 8·22·8

___ ___ ___ ___   ___ ___ ___   ___ ___ ___ ___ ___ ___

What did the owl write to her sweetheart?

12·4·15   26·15·4·26·2·8   25·22

___ ___ ___   ___ ___ ___ ___ ___ ___   ___ ___

2·12·6·9   5·26·15·22·13·7·18·13·22

___ ___ ___ ___   ___ ___ ___ ___ ___ ___ ___ ___ ___

What did the bee say to his sweetheart?

2·12·6 9·22   26   19·12·13·22·2

___ ___ ___ ___ ___ ,   ___   ___ ___ ___ ___ ___

12·21   26   5·26·15·22·13·7·18·13·22

___ ___   ___   ___ ___ ___ ___ ___ ___ ___ ___ ___!

Seasonal Activities

Mend These Broken Hearts

Select the three words that go together to create a set. Write the words in the correct heart. You may need to use a dictionary!

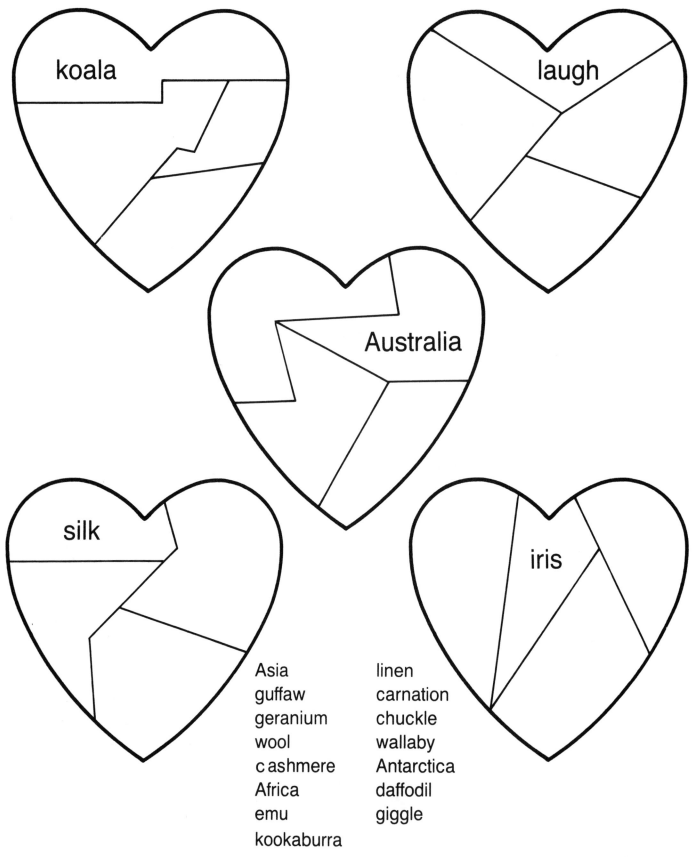

koala

laugh

Australia

silk

iris

Asia   linen
guffaw   carnation
geranium   chuckle
wool   wallaby
cashmere   Antarctica
Africa   daffodil
emu   giggle
kookaburra

Write Your Own Valentine Rhymes

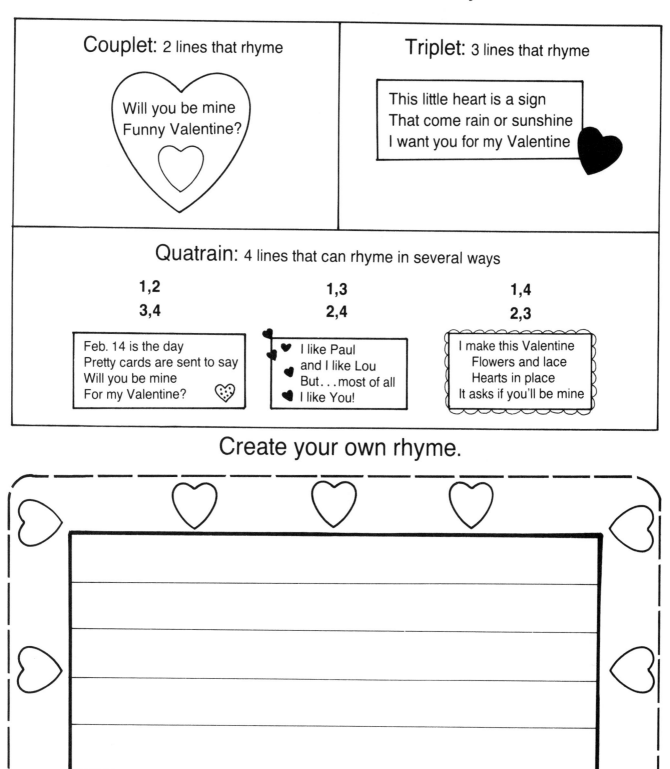

Couplet: 2 lines that rhyme

Will you be mine
Funny Valentine?

Triplet: 3 lines that rhyme

This little heart is a sign
That come rain or sunshine
I want you for my Valentine

Quatrain: 4 lines that can rhyme in several ways

| 1,2 | 1,3 | 1,4 |
| 3,4 | 2,4 | 2,3 |

Feb. 14 is the day
Pretty cards are sent to say
Will you be mine
For my Valentine?

I like Paul
and I like Lou
But...most of all
I like You!

I make this Valentine
Flowers and lace
Hearts in place
It asks if you'll be mine

Create your own rhyme.

Give it to a special friend.

Find the Valentine Message

_____ February
_____ lace
_____ candy
_____ party
_____ love
_____ note
_____ pink
_____ friend
_____ heart
_____ card
_____ merry
_____ tulips
_____ flowers

1. month after January
2. blossoms like daffodils
3. happy; cheerful
4. sweets like chocolate
5. special friendship; affection
6. a greeting sent through the mail
7. cup-shaped flowers
8. the shape of Valentines
9. a pal; someone you enjoy being with
10. a celebration
11. mix red and white to get _____
12. a short letter
13. a delicate edging used on clothes for decoration

What is the secret message?

_____

Seasonal Activities

February

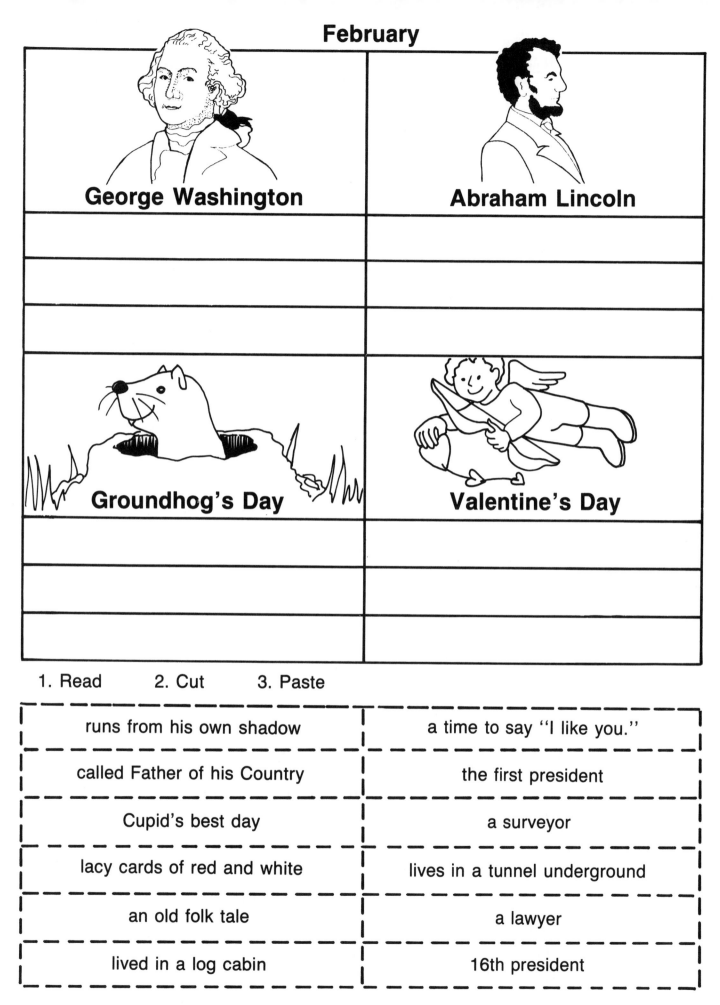

George Washington	Abraham Lincoln
Groundhog's Day	Valentine's Day

1. Read   2. Cut   3. Paste

runs from his own shadow	a time to say "I like you."
called Father of his Country	the first president
Cupid's best day	a surveyor
lacy cards of red and white	lives in a tunnel underground
an old folk tale	a lawyer
lived in a log cabin	16th president

               Seasonal Activities

George Washington and Abraham Lincoln

_____

Write these facts next to the correct picture:

1st president of the USA

16th president of the USA

called "Honest Abe"

called "Father of his Country"

was a farmer and surveyor

was a rail-splitter and lawyer

born in Virginia on Feb. 22, 1732

born in Kentucky on Feb. 12, 1809

his family plantation was called Mt. Vernon

he grew up in a log cabin

married Martha Dandridge

married Mary Todd

General in the Revolutionary War

President during the Civil War

shot and killed in 1865

died of illness in 1799

1. Cut out a picture.   2. Paste it to lined paper.   3. Write.

Search For The Presidents

```
K M E N W I L S O N E M A C L
H A C I A F T Y L E R C S L G
A D A M S M O N R O E K H E A
R I R E H E T R O P D I J V R
D S T V I E N A D R O N A E F
I O E A N N I H Y A T L C L I
N N R N G R E G O L L E K A E
G F F S T A F T R W O Y S N L
P I O N O L S O N A E R O D D
I L L I N C O L N S N R N I E
E L W X R E A G A N A T I N A
R M H O O V E R J O H N S O N
C O I N O A R T T R U M A N M
E R S U S N B U C H A N A N U
J E F F E R S O N A R T H U R
A L D O V A N B U R E N E A R
K E N N E D Y I H A Y E S H Y
E M I L L E R C O O L I D G E
G I L L T H A R R I S O N S O
```

____ Adams
____ Arthur
____ Buchanan
____ Carter
____ Cleveland
____ Coolidge
____ Eisenhower
____ Fillmore
____ Ford

____ Garfield
____ Grant
____ Harding
____ Harrison
____ Hayes
____ Hoover
____ Jackson
____ Jefferson
____ Johnson

____ Kennedy
____ Lincoln
____ Madison
____ McKinley
____ Monroe
____ Nixon
____ Pierce
____ Polk
____ Reagan

____ Roosevelt
____ Taft
____ Taylor
____ Truman
____ Tyler
____ VanBuren
____ Washington
____ Wilson

Seasonal Activities

A Visit to Washington D.C.

Poll 20 people.
Ask them the following two questions.
Record their answers on graphs A and B.

A. Have you ever visited Washington, D.C.?

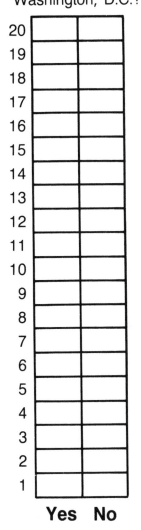

| | Yes | No |

B. Did you see any of these buildings?

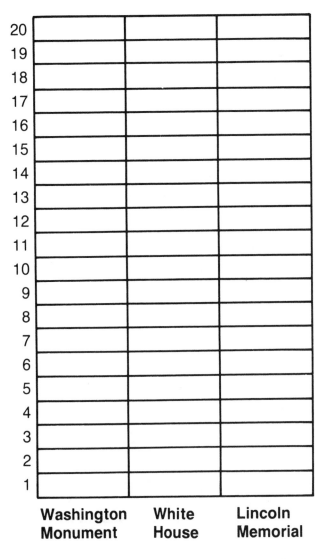

| Washington Monument | White House | Lincoln Memorial |

Seasonal Activities

Use the code to decipher the names of these famous American sights. Paste the correct picture by each name.

★★★

1	2	3	4	5	6	7	8	9	10	11	12	13	14	15	16	17	18	19	20	21	22	23	24	25	26
A	B	C	D	E	F	G	H	I	J	K	L	M	N	O	P	Q	R	S	T	U	V	W	X	Y	Z

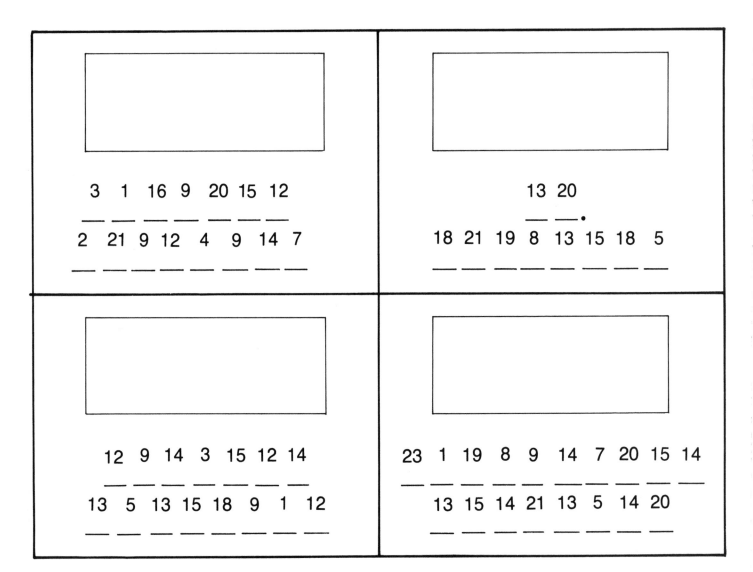

3 1 16 9 20 15 12
— — — — — — —
2 21 9 12 4 9 14 7
— — — — — — — —

13 20
— —.
18 21 19 8 13 15 18 5
— — — — — — — —

12 9 14 3 15 12 14
— — — — — — —
13 5 13 15 18 9 1 12
— — — — — — — —

23 1 19 8 9 14 7 20 15 14
— — — — — — — — — —
13 15 14 21 13 5 14 20
— — — — — — — —

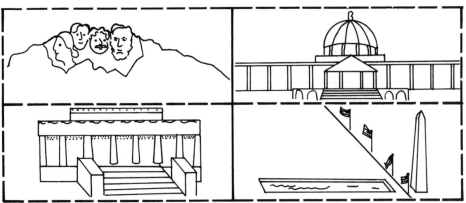

Seasonal Activities

Spring Activities

Seasonal Activities

Name It

	flower	something you can buy in a store	something to eat or drink	describing word	boy's name
example **L**	lily	lock	lemonade	lumpy	Larry
S					
P					
R					
I					
N					
G					

March	year	The season is: winter summer spring fall

Sunday	Monday	Tuesday	Wednesday	Thursday	Friday	Saturday

1. Write the number for each day in March.
2. There are always _____ days in March.
3. Draw a beautiful flower on the first day of spring.
4. List the date of each Friday in March.

_____

_____

5. Draw a shamrock on Saint Patrick's Day.
6. Record class birthdays on your calendar.

Turn this paper over and draw a leprechaun hiding his pot of gold under a mushroom.

	year	The season is:
April		winter summer spring fall

Sunday	Monday	Tuesday	Wednesday	Thursday	Friday	Saturday

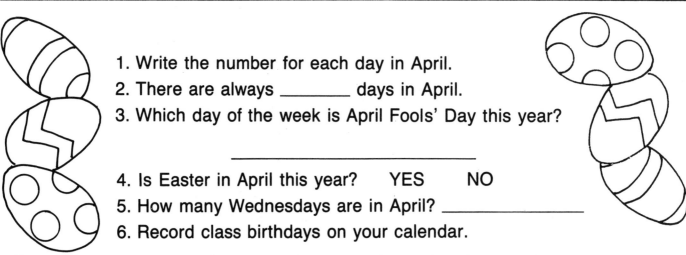

1. Write the number for each day in April.
2. There are always _____ days in April.
3. Which day of the week is April Fools' Day this year?

   _____

4. Is Easter in April this year?   YES   NO
5. How many Wednesdays are in April? _____
6. Record class birthdays on your calendar.

Turn this paper over and make a picture to show what the weather is like today (windy, sunny ...).

 Seasonal Activities

| | | May | year | | The season is:

winter   summer
spring   fall |

Sunday	Monday	Tuesday	Wednesday	Thursday	Friday	Saturday

1. Write the number for each day in May.
2. There are always _____ days in May.
3. Outline Mother's Day with your favorite color.
4. Draw a basket of spring flowers on May Day.
5. May 18th is the day of the Jumping Frog Contest in Calaveras County, California. Make a little green frog on May 18th.
6. Record class birthdays on your calendar.

Turn this paper over and make a picture of your mother.

March Winds and April Showers

Find the hidden weather words.

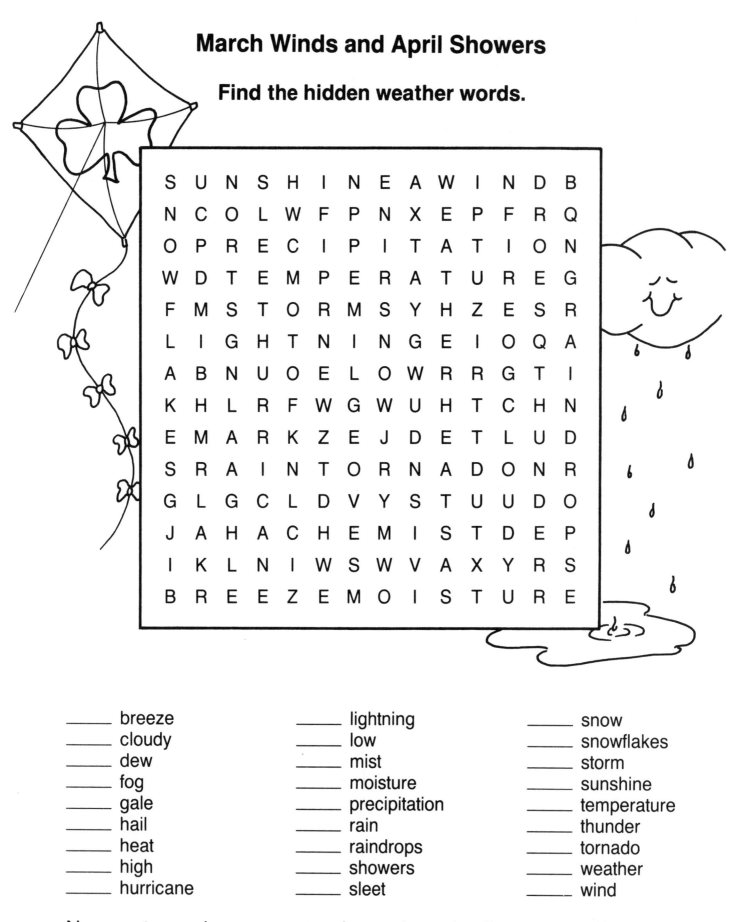

```
S U N S H I N E A W I N D B
N C O L W F P N X E P F R Q
O P R E C I P I T A T I O N
W D T E M P E R A T U R E G
F M S T O R M S Y H Z E S R
L I G H T N I N G E I O Q A
A B N U O E L O W R R G T I
K H L R F W G W U H T C H N
E M A R K Z E J D E T L U D
S R A I N T O R N A D O N R
G L G C L D V Y S T U U D O
J A H A C H E M I S T D E P
I K L N I W S W V A X Y R S
B R E E Z E M O I S T U R E
```

_____ breeze   _____ lightning   _____ snow
_____ cloudy   _____ low   _____ snowflakes
_____ dew   _____ mist   _____ storm
_____ fog   _____ moisture   _____ sunshine
_____ gale   _____ precipitation   _____ temperature
_____ hail   _____ rain   _____ thunder
_____ heat   _____ raindrops   _____ tornado
_____ high   _____ showers   _____ weather
_____ hurricane   _____ sleet   _____ wind

Now, put a red x next to each word on the list that describes
SPRING weather.

         Seasonal Activities

March Puzzle Fun

1. precious metal
2. the "Emerald Isle"
3. another name for a pan
4. Saint _____
5. wear this color on St. Patrick's Day
6. the month after February

7. a "good luck" leaf
8. good to eat boiled, mashed or fried
9. a Leprechaun's gold is his _____
10. March _____s help you to fly kites

Word Box				
wind	shamrock	potatoes	Ireland	treasure
gold	Patrick	pot	green	March

Draw the mystery creature on the back of this paper.

105   Seasonal Activities

March

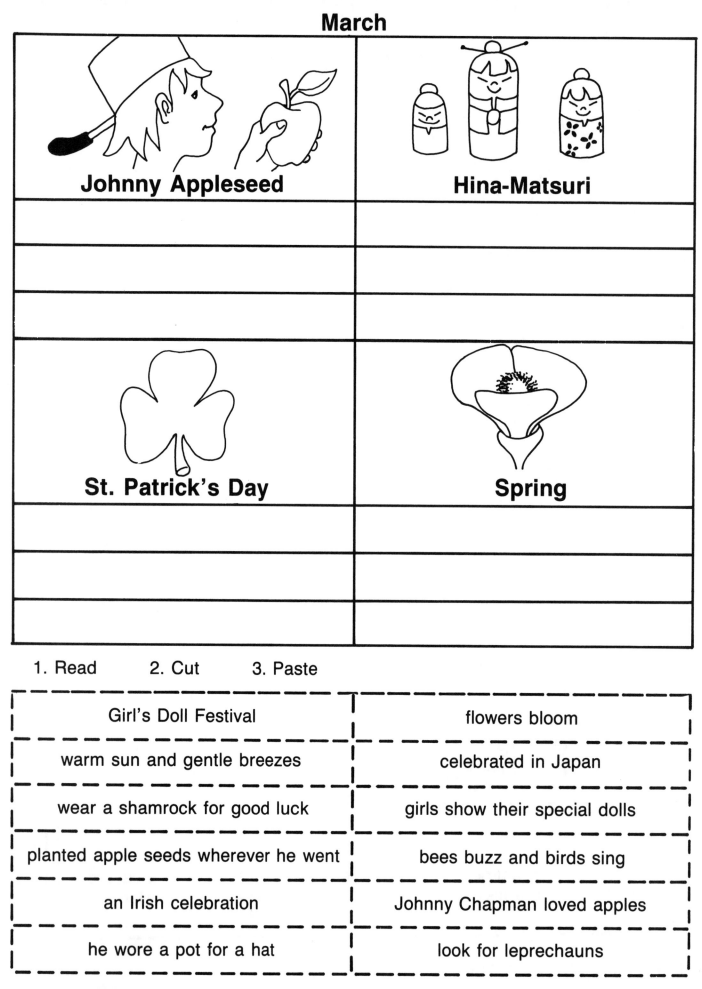

Johnny Appleseed

Hina-Matsuri

St. Patrick's Day

Spring

1. Read   2. Cut   3. Paste

Girl's Doll Festival	flowers bloom
warm sun and gentle breezes	celebrated in Japan
wear a shamrock for good luck	girls show their special dolls
planted apple seeds wherever he went	bees buzz and birds sing
an Irish celebration	Johnny Chapman loved apples
he wore a pot for a hat	look for leprechauns

Seasonal Activities

Write a verse about kites.

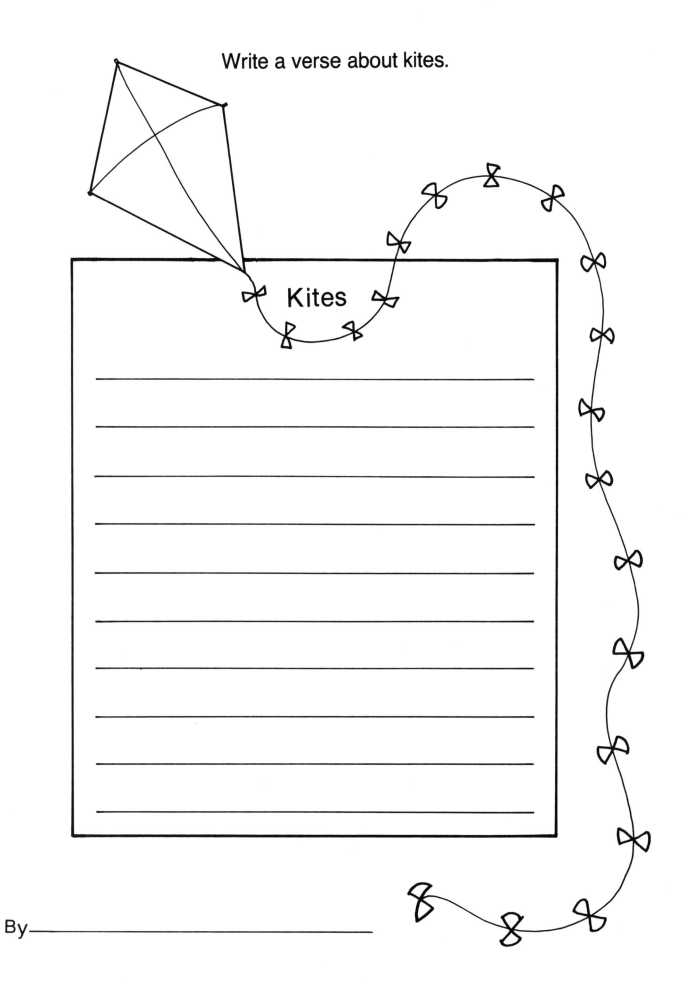

Kites

_____

_____

_____

_____

_____

_____

_____

_____

_____

By_____

 Seasonal Activities

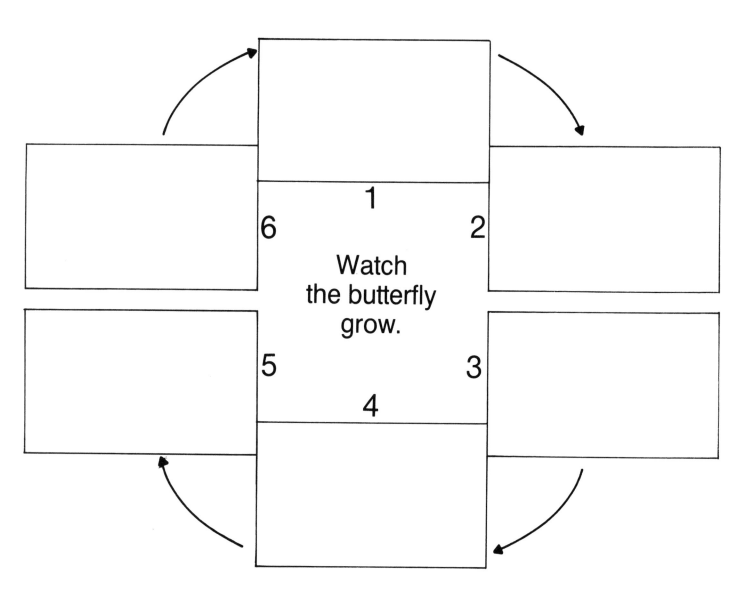

	1	
6	Watch the butterfly grow.	2
5		3
	4	

Cut and paste in order.

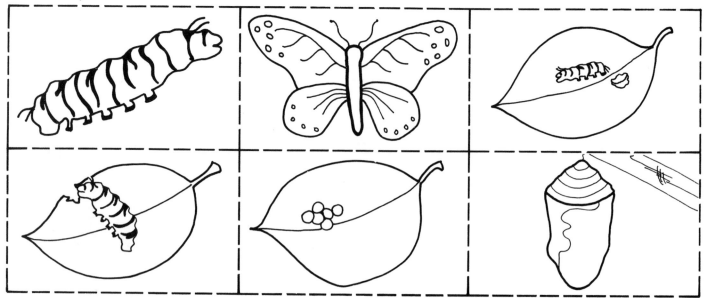

Seasonal Activities

Butterfly Shape Poems

1. Draw.
   Get a piece of paper.
   Use a crayon or pen.
   Draw only the outline of
   the butterfly.

small
colorful
curly tongue
can fly
antennae
beautiful
tiny scales
soft
sips nectar

2. Describe the butterfly.
   Get a piece of writing
   paper. Make a list of
   words or phrases about
   the butterfly. Arrange
   them in a way that
   sounds pleasing to you.

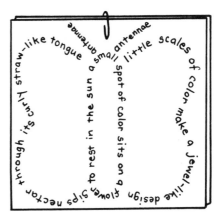

3. Get a sheet of plain
   paper. Put the paper
   over your drawing. Clip
   the papers together with
   a paper clip so they
   won't wiggle. Write your
   description following the
   shape of the picture.

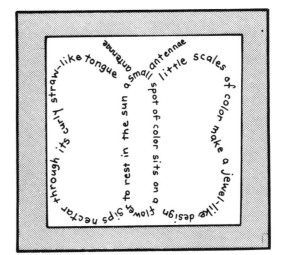

4. Get a sheet of colored
   paper. Paste your poem
   to the paper to make a
   frame.

109   Seasonal Activities

Color. Cut out. Paste to blue paper.

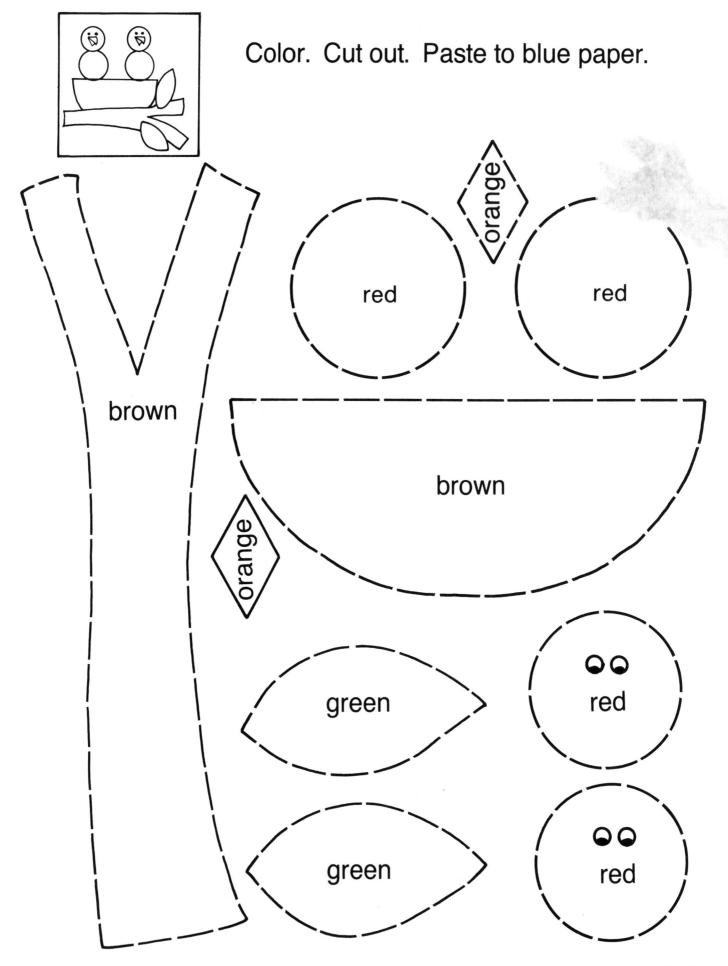

red

orange

red

brown

brown

orange

green

red

green

red

Seasonal Activities

Write a cinquain for spring.

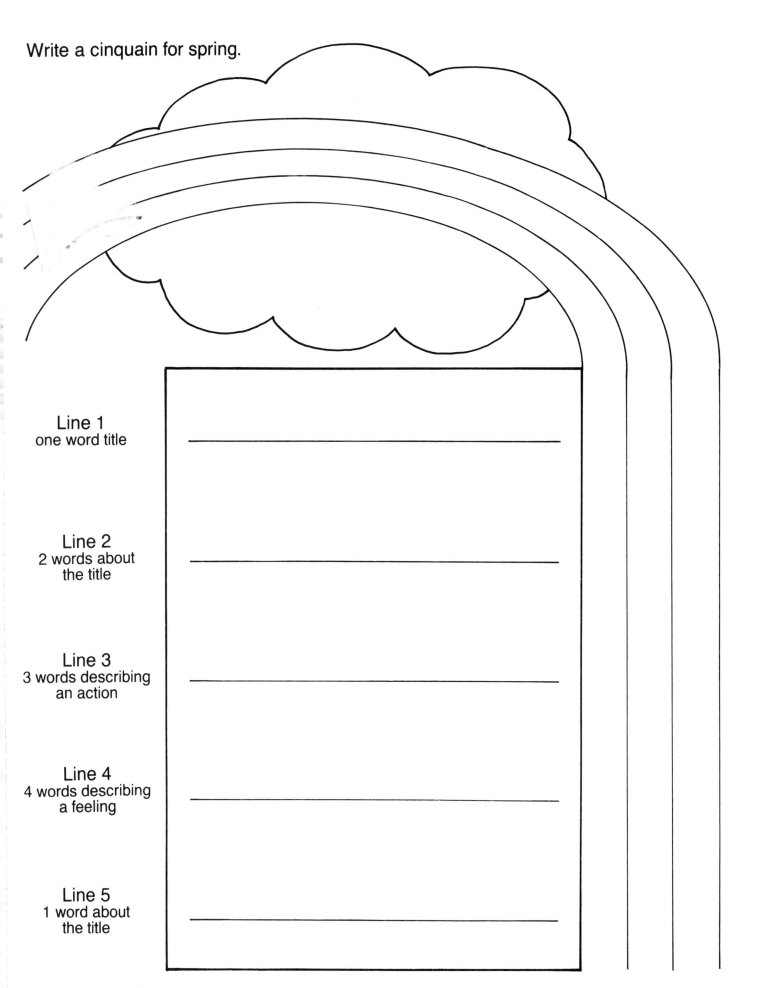

Line 1
one word title

_____

Line 2
2 words about
the title

_____

Line 3
3 words describing
an action

_____

Line 4
4 words describing
a feeling

_____

Line 5
1 word about
the title

_____

Seasonal Activities

In _____'s Flower Basket

your name

Unscramble the flower names.
Write each name on the correct blossom.

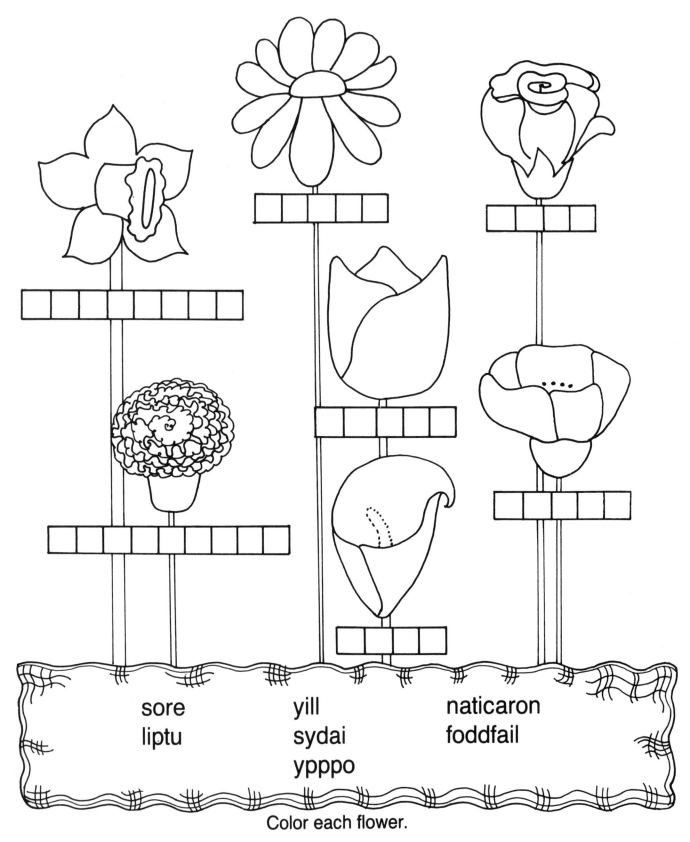

sore   yill   naticaron

liptu   sydai   foddfail

ypppo

Color each flower.

Seasonal Activities

1. Cut.   2. Paste to lined paper.   3. Write.

113   Seasonal Activities

How Does Your Garden Grow?

Jack planted a magic bean seed and climbed to the clouds for an exciting adventure. Here is your magic seed. Draw a picture to show what will grow. Then get a sheet of paper and describe your own adventure.

Paste your picture to the top of your story.

 Seasonal Activities

Aunt Mollie's Flower Garden

Aunt Mollie is ready to start planting her spring flower garden, but she spilled all her seed and bulb packages. Now they are so mixed up that she can't find which seeds she wants to use. You can help make her job easier by putting them in alphabetical order.

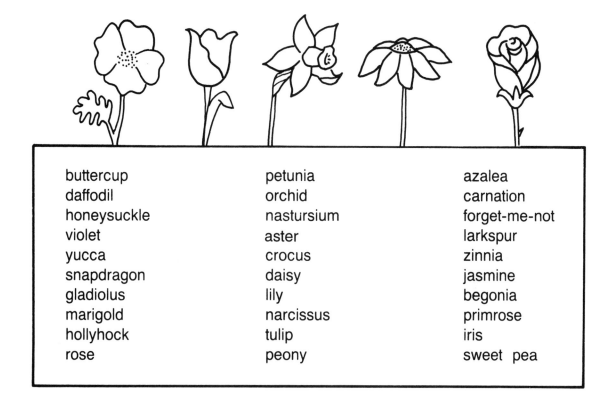

buttercup	petunia	azalea
daffodil	orchid	carnation
honeysuckle	nastursium	forget-me-not
violet	aster	larkspur
yucca	crocus	zinnia
snapdragon	daisy	jasmine
gladiolus	lily	begonia
marigold	narcissus	primrose
hollyhock	tulip	iris
rose	peony	sweet pea

1. _____
2. _____
3. _____
4. _____
5. _____
6. _____
7. _____
8. _____
9. _____
10. _____
11. _____
12. _____
13. _____
14. _____
15. _____
16. _____
17. _____
18. _____
19. _____
20. _____
21. _____
22. _____
23. _____
24. _____
25. _____
26. _____
27. _____
28. _____
29. _____
30. _____

Aunt Mollie says, "Thanks for your help!"

Seasonal Activities

Connect the dots to see who is on the nest.
Count by 2's.

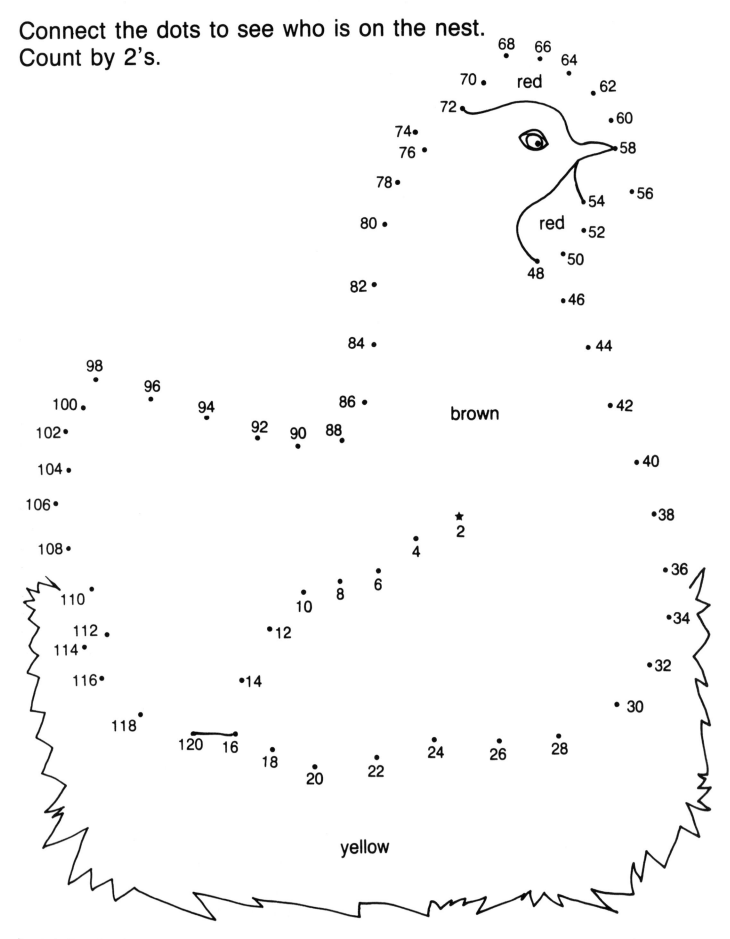

Seasonal Activities

Drawing Fun

Who is sitting under this mushroom?
Follow the steps and draw the surprise in the box.

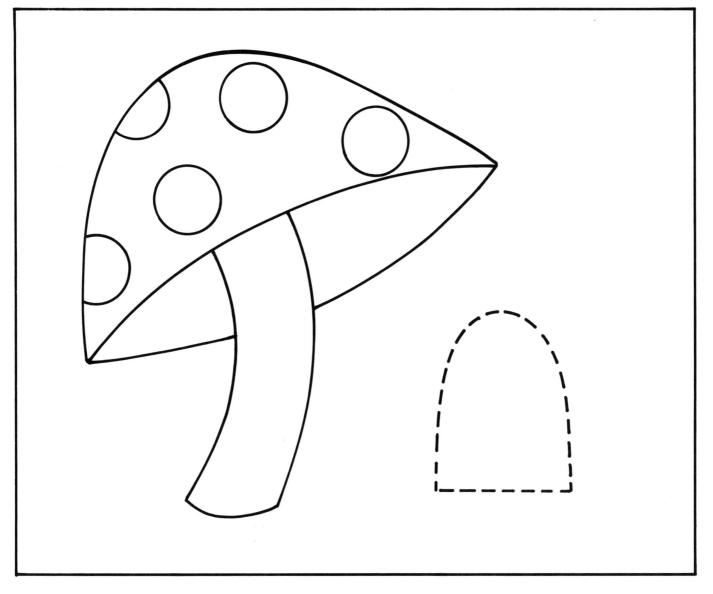

1. Follow the drawing steps.

2. Color the leprechaun's suit green. Make his hair orange.
3. Add a pot of gold next to the leprechaun. Put a shamrock in his hat.

 Seasonal Activities

Categories

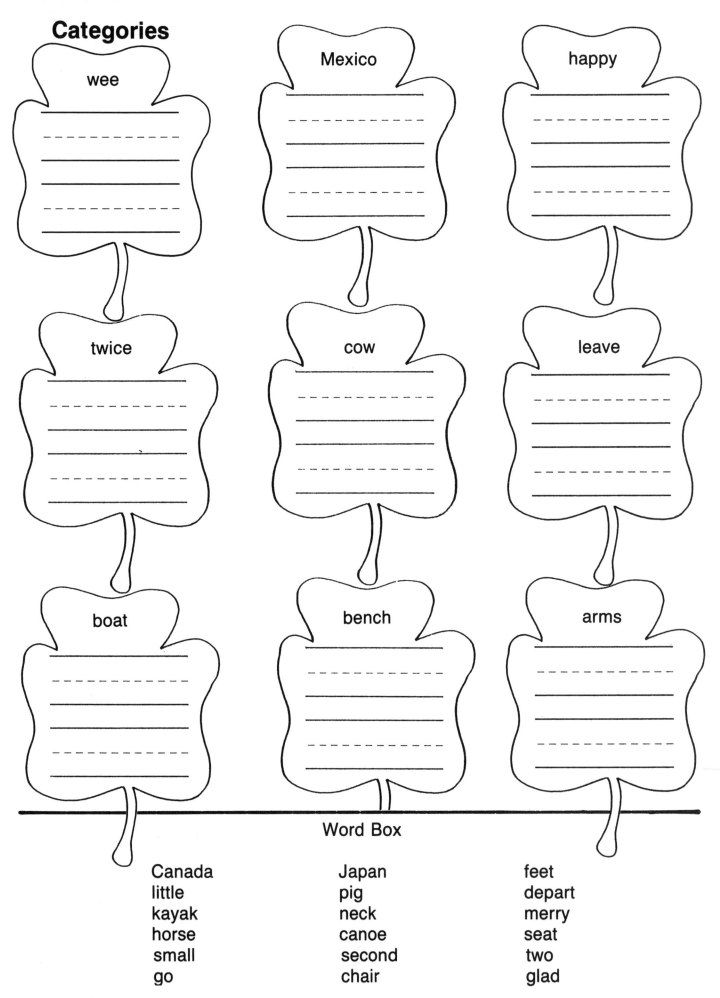

wee

Mexico

happy

twice

cow

leave

boat

bench

arms

Word Box

Canada	Japan	feet
little	pig	depart
kayak	neck	merry
horse	canoe	seat
small	second	two
go	chair	glad

Seasonal Activities

April

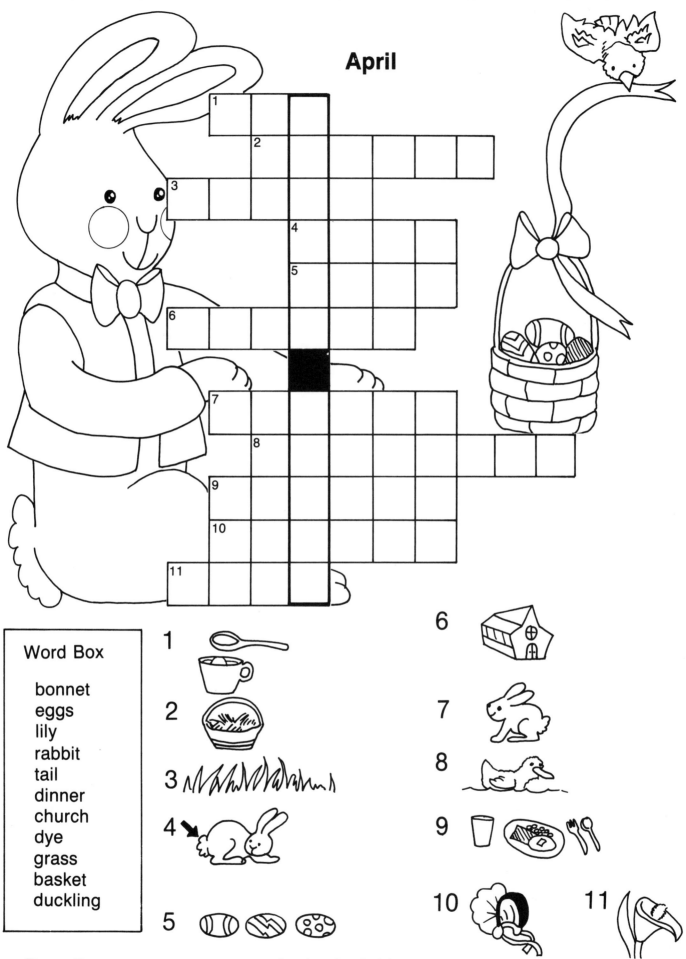

Word Box

bonnet
eggs
lily
rabbit
tail
dinner
church
dye
grass
basket
duckling

Draw the mystery creature on the back of this paper.

Seasonal Activities

Mushroom Mysteries

Paste the riddle to the top of the mushroom it answers.

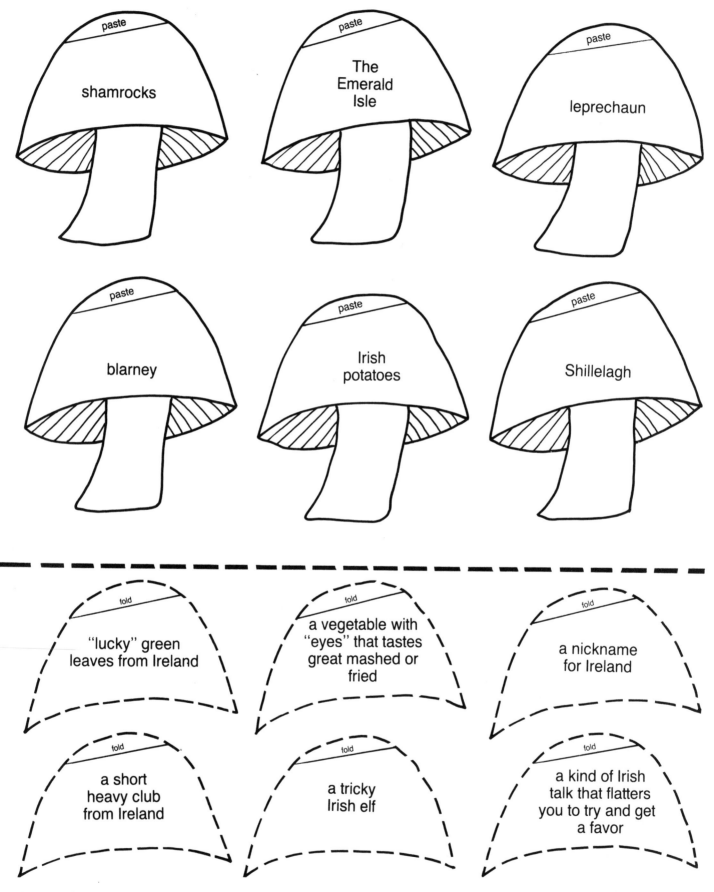

shamrocks

The Emerald Isle

leprechaun

blarney

Irish potatoes

Shillelagh

"lucky" green leaves from Ireland

a vegetable with "eyes" that tastes great mashed or fried

a nickname for Ireland

a short heavy club from Ireland

a tricky Irish elf

a kind of Irish talk that flatters you to try and get a favor

Seasonal Activities

My Lucky Shamrock
What can it be?

Write a wish on each section...

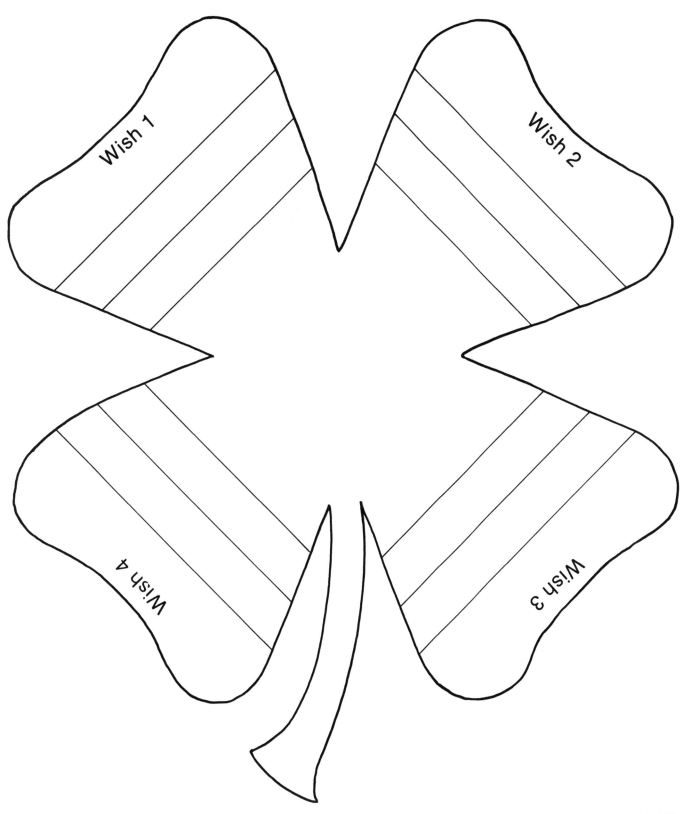

Wish 1

Wish 2

Wish 4

Wish 3

Seasonal Activities

Complete the leprechaun   Color.

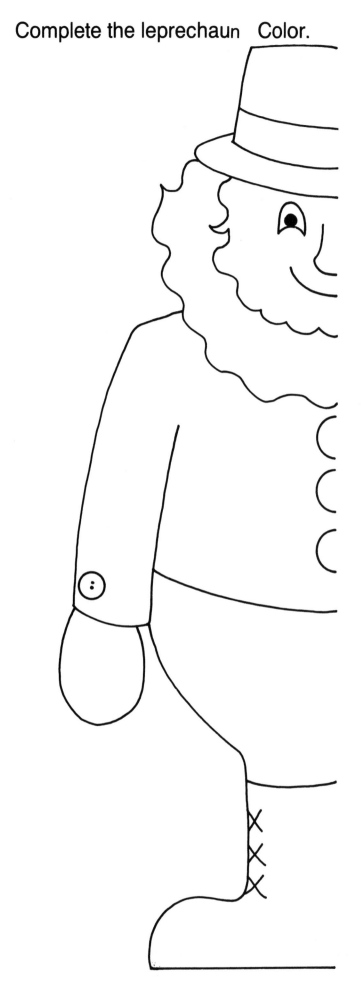

Help the Leprechaun find the hidden words.

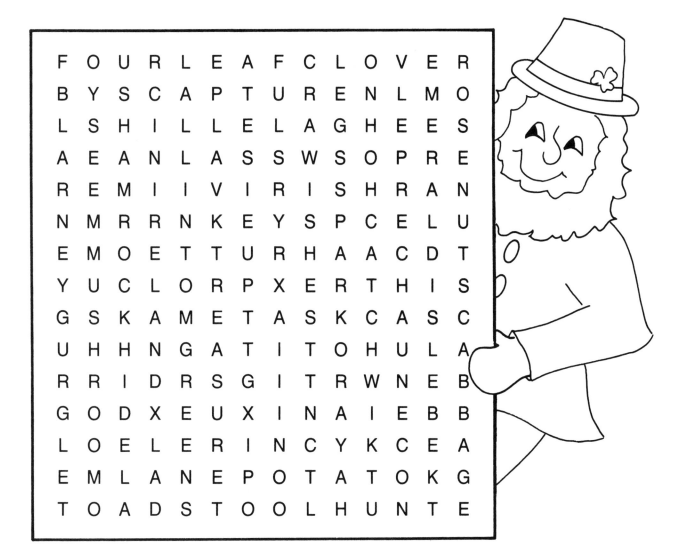

```
F O U R L E A F C L O V E R
B Y S C A P T U R E N L M O
L S H I L L E L A G H E E S
A E A N L A S S W S O P R E
R E M I I V I R I S H R A N
N M R R N K E Y S P C E L U
E M O E T T U R H A A C D T
Y U C L O R P X E R T H I S
G S K A M E T A S K C A S C
U H H N G A T I T O H U L A
R R I D R S G I T R W N E B
G O D X E U X I N A I E B B
L O E L E R I N C Y K C E A
E M L A N E P O T A T O K G
T O A D S T O O L H U N T E
```

blarney	hide	potato
cabbage	hunt	Saint Patrick
capture	Ireland	shamrock
catch	Irish	shillelagh
Emerald Isle	lad	silver
Erin	lass	tiny
four-leaf clover	Leprechaun	toadstool
gold	magic	treasure
green	mushroom	wee
		wishes

Can you find any other words? _____ If yes, how many? _____

Seasonal Activities

Story Starters

1. Choose a story starter.
2. Paste it to the top of a sheet of paper.
3. Write!
4. Draw a picture to go with your story.

All his life Timothy had heard that leprechauns hide their fortunes. He was determined to locate some of that treasure. All he had to do was capture one of the tiny green fellows.

I never realized how exciting my family's vacation in Ireland was going to be, until. . .

One spring evening, Tonya spied a wee leprechaun racing across her backyard. She. . .

Seasonal Activities

Riddle Time

Use the Morse code to solve these riddles.

A ·—	E ·	I ··	M ——	Q ——·—	U ··—	Y —·——
B —···	F ··—·	J ·———	N —·	R ·—·	V ···—	Z ——··
C —·—·	G ——·	K —·—	O ———	S ···	W ·——	
D —··	H ····	L ·—··	P ·——·	T —	X —··—	

1. How does a leprechaun make gold soup?

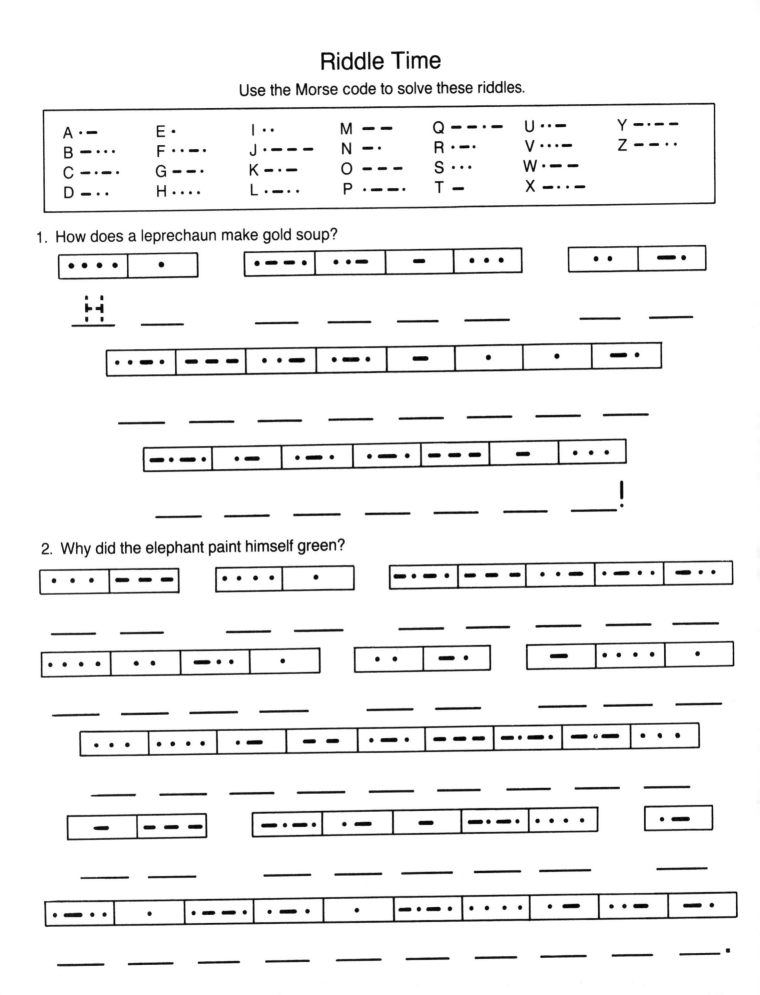

2. Why did the elephant paint himself green?

Put this picture together to find out what the bunny is doing.

Cut and paste.

Opposites

work

_____

- - - - - - - - -

_____

whisper

_____

- - - - - - - - -

_____

full

_____

- - - - - - - - -

_____

hard

_____

- - - - - - - - -

_____

long

_____

- - - - - - - - -

_____

over

_____

- - - - - - - - -

_____

many

_____

- - - - - - - - -

_____

fat

_____

- - - - - - - - -

_____

loud

_____

- - - - - - - - -

_____

laugh

_____

- - - - - - - - -

_____

open

_____

- - - - - - - - -

_____

day

_____

- - - - - - - - -

_____

off

_____

- - - - - - - - -

_____

hello

_____

- - - - - - - - -

_____

dry

_____

- - - - - - - - -

_____

Word Box				
empty	wet	good-bye	night	yell
under	few	short	on	shut
cry	thin	play	quiet	soft

Seasonal Activities

Circle each word in the puzzle as you find it.
You will find words across, down and diagonally.
A few words are written backwards.

Easter Hunt

```
C D L R M A R C H E A M X T
Y Z O V D E C O R A T E R F
A J Z S U N D A Y S U T S T
S R B M C G H U N T V F H R
K L U N K P F L L E K W O T
L F N N L P L A P R I L W A
L S N P I O O C Z A X G E W
T D Y E N B W C H Y N J R A
E P C N G W E B L I I R S L
R M D E U G R C R U C D A Y
P N G R A S S P G H I K U B
B A O V B A S K E T H R E Y
```

Cross out each word as you find it.

	dye	
April	Easter	hunt
basket	eggs	March
bunny	flowers	spring
chick	grass	Sunday
decorate	showers	duckling

Seasonal Activities

1. Color the hare.
2. Cut out all pieces.
3. Put the pieces together with brass fasteners.

A Dancing Hare

Easter Crossword

Across

2. a spring holiday
4. plant daffodil _____ in the garden
5. send a greeting _____
8. change something from plain to fancy
11. another name for rabbit
12. an Easter hat
14. Easter flowers
15. a green plant covering the ground
16. to look for something

Down

1. to hunt
3. day of the week
4. a container with a handle
6. change the color of something
7. people go to _____ on Sundays
9. another name for bunny
10. a sign for a church
13. hens lay _____

Word Box:

basket	Easter
bonnet	eggs
bulbs	grass
bunny	hunt
card	lilies
church	rabbit
cross	search
decorate	Sunday
dye	

Seasonal Activities

Complete the chick in its egg. Color.

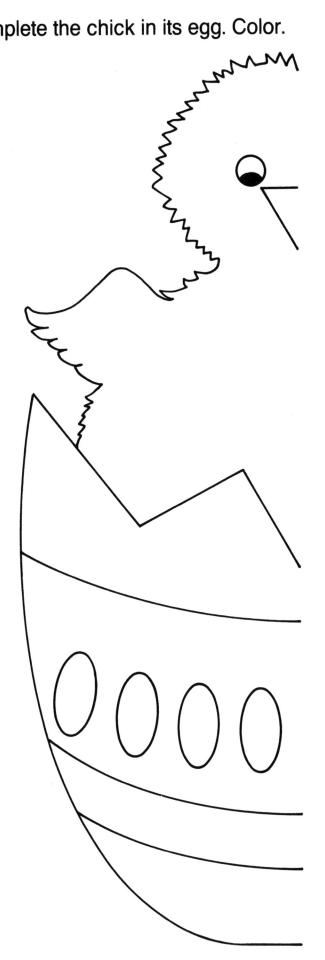

131

Seasonal Activities

Connect the dots. Count by 2's.

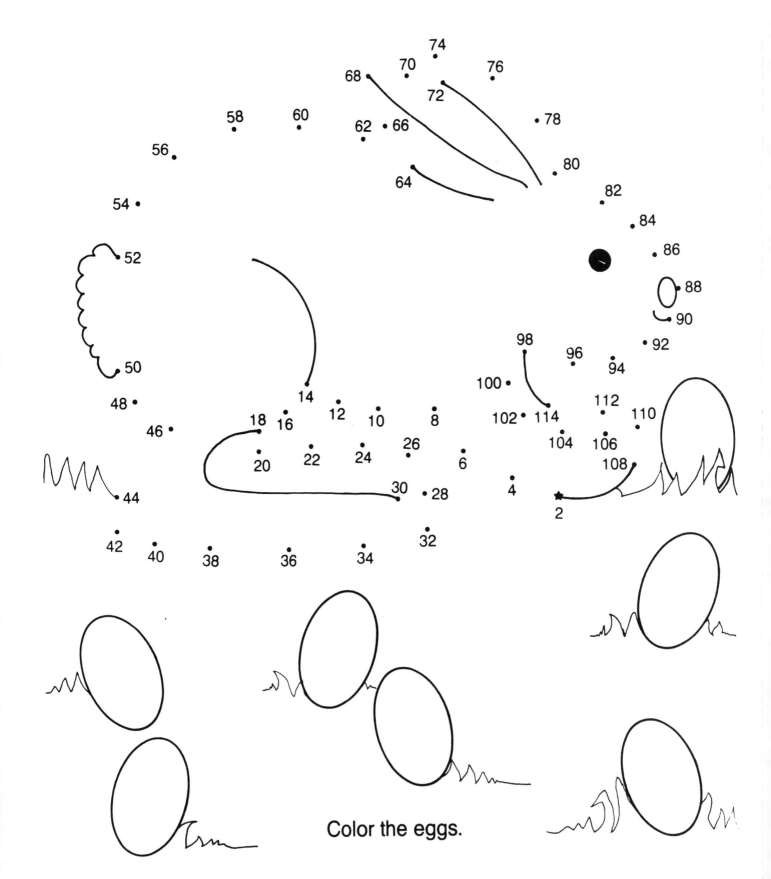

Color the eggs.

An Easter Surprise

1 moo	baa	clang	buzz / ten	splash	peep / zero	ouch	quack	woof
2 snake	dog	zebra	owl	man	duck	cow	moose	fish
3 Maine	Atlantic	Idaho	Mars / Iowa	Florida	Earth / Texas	Alaska	Pacific	Montana
4 orange	milk	apple	plum / roast	fig / potato	pear / steak	cherry	juice	banana
5 fork	book	pan / log	window	table	bottle	nail / desk	letter	knife
6 feather	toes	fin	mane	gills	hoof	scale	finger	beak
7 tree	buffalo	pig	elk	toad	poodle	duck	whale	carrot
8 rose	worm	dog	monkey	eel	horse	fish	mule	tulip
9 grass	bear	swan	cat	cow	parrot	hen	hippo	cactus
10 bush	bee / weed	deer	mice	moose	canary	frog	ant / corn	vine

Color:

Row 1: sounds-blue
numbers-red

Row 2: 4 legs-brown
2 legs-red
0 legs-blue

Row 3: planets-red
oceans-brown
states-blue

Row 4: fruit-blue
vegetables-yellow
meat-green
things to drink-brown

Row 5: wood-yellow
metal-blue
glass-green
paper-brown

Row 6: parts of a:
horse-green
fish-yellow
bird-blue
person-brown

Rows 7-10: animals-brown
plants-blue

An *Eggs...tra* Special Word Search

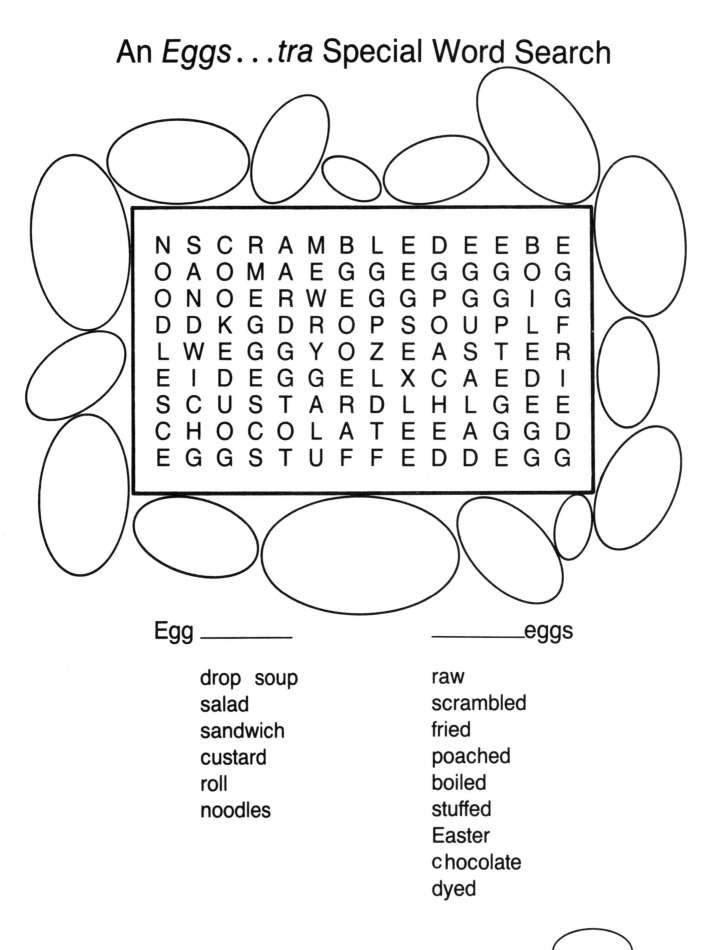

```
N  S  C  R  A  M  B  L  E  D  E  E  B  E
O  A  O  M  A  E  G  G  E  G  G  G  O  G
O  N  O  E  R  W  E  G  G  P  G  G  I  G
D  D  K  G  D  R  O  P  S  O  U  P  L  F
L  W  E  G  G  Y  O  Z  E  A  S  T  E  R
E  I  D  E  G  G  E  L  X  C  A  E  D  I
S  C  U  S  T  A  R  D  L  H  L  G  E  E
C  H  O  C  O  L  A  T  E  E  A  G  G  D
E  G  G  S  T  U  F  F  E  D  D  D  E  G  G
```

Egg _____   _____ eggs

drop soup	raw
salad	scrambled
sandwich	fried
custard	poached
roll	boiled
noodles	stuffed
	Easter
	chocolate
	dyed

NOW...how many times can you find **egg**?

134   Seasonal Activities

Help Humpty Dumpty put the eggs together.

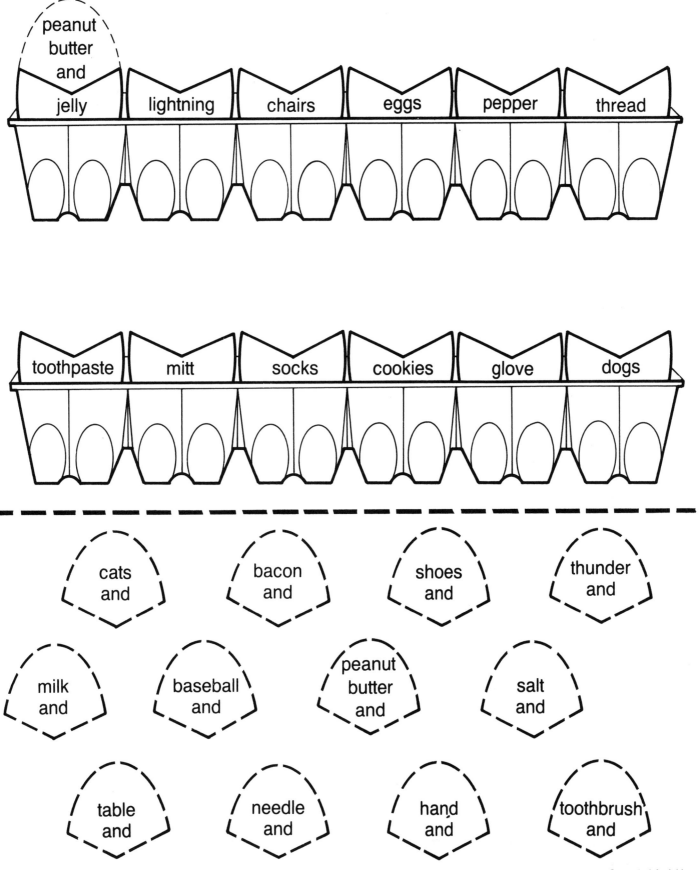

peanut butter and jelly · lightning · chairs · eggs · pepper · thread

toothpaste · mitt · socks · cookies · glove · dogs

cats and · bacon and · shoes and · thunder and

milk and · baseball and · peanut butter and · salt and

table and · needle and · hand and · toothbrush and

Seasonal Activities

Take a peek under the eggs.

Write an Easter story on your paper.

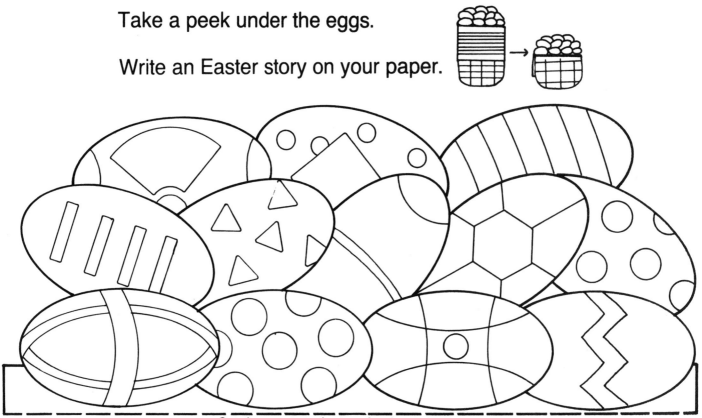

Cut, then paste to the top of a sheet of paper.

Cut, then paste to the bottom of the sheet of paper.

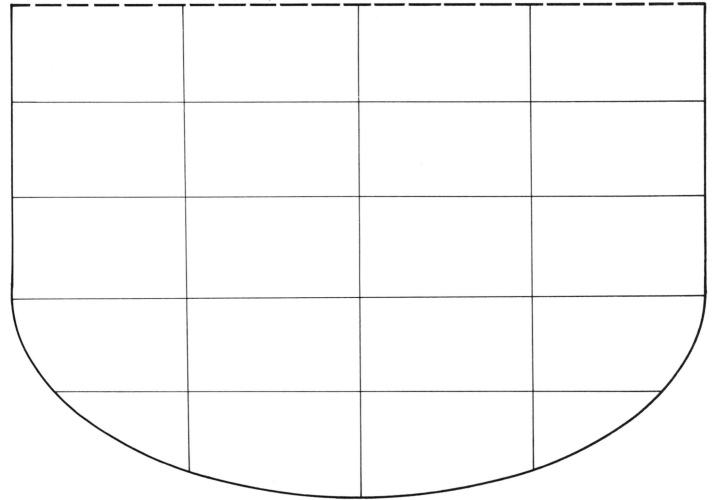

Bunny Tales

1. Choose a title. Copy it on your writing paper.
2. Put your imagination to work.
3. Write a special story.
4. Illustrate your story.

The Forgetful Easter Bunny
Peter Cottontail's First Easter
Arturo and the Mysterious Egg
How the Easter Bunny Gets His Egg
If I Were the Easter Rabbit
Tammy and the Magic Basket
In My Easter Basket
The Substitute Easter Bunny

 Seasonal Activities

Pysanky Eggs

Ukrainian Easter eggs are decorated with symbols of good wishes.
These beautiful eggs are then given to special friends and family
members. Here are some of the symbols used and what they mean:

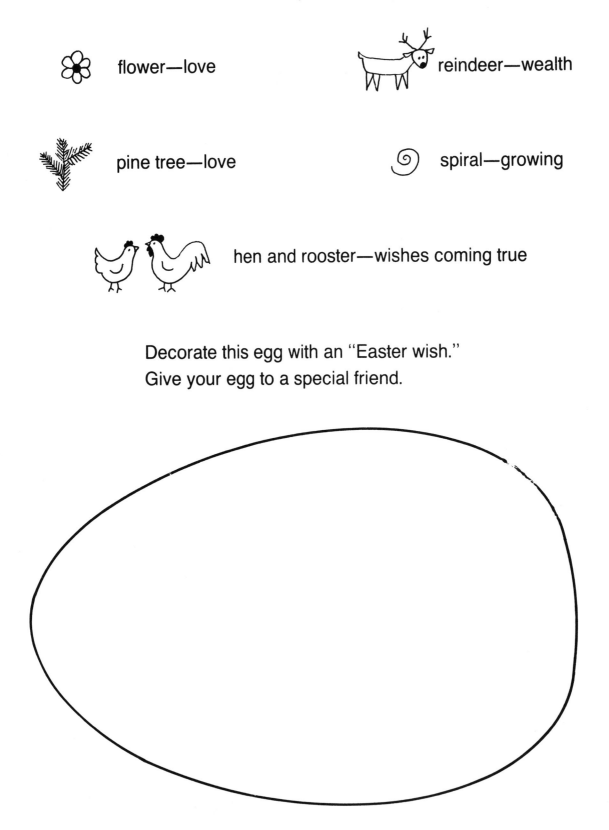

flower—love

reindeer—wealth

pine tree—love

spiral—growing

hen and rooster—wishes coming true

Decorate this egg with an "Easter wish."
Give your egg to a special friend.

Seasonal Activities

Unscramble the Eggs

Help Mr. Rabbit decorate the Easter eggs.

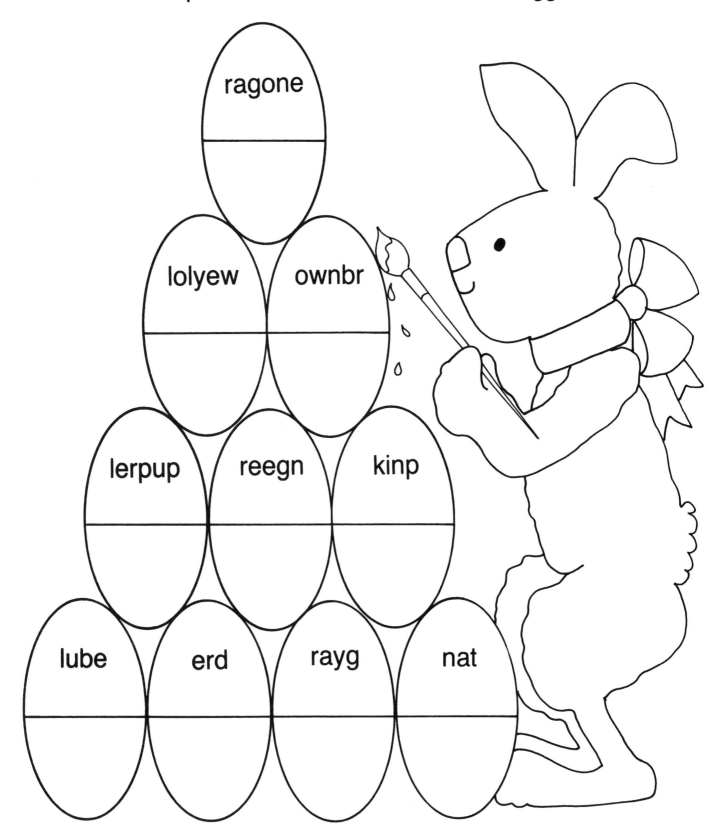

ragone

lolyew   ownbr

lerpup   reegn   kinp

lube   erd   rayg   nat

How to Dye an Easter Egg

Color the picture.

1.

2.

3.

4.

- -

Cut. Paste in order.

Put eggs in the cups. Turn the eggs with a spoon.

Get cups and spoons. Set them on the table.

Lift the eggs out and let them dry.

Put dye in each cup. Add water and vinegar. Stir.

Seasonal Activities

A Rabbit Fantasy—Read and Draw

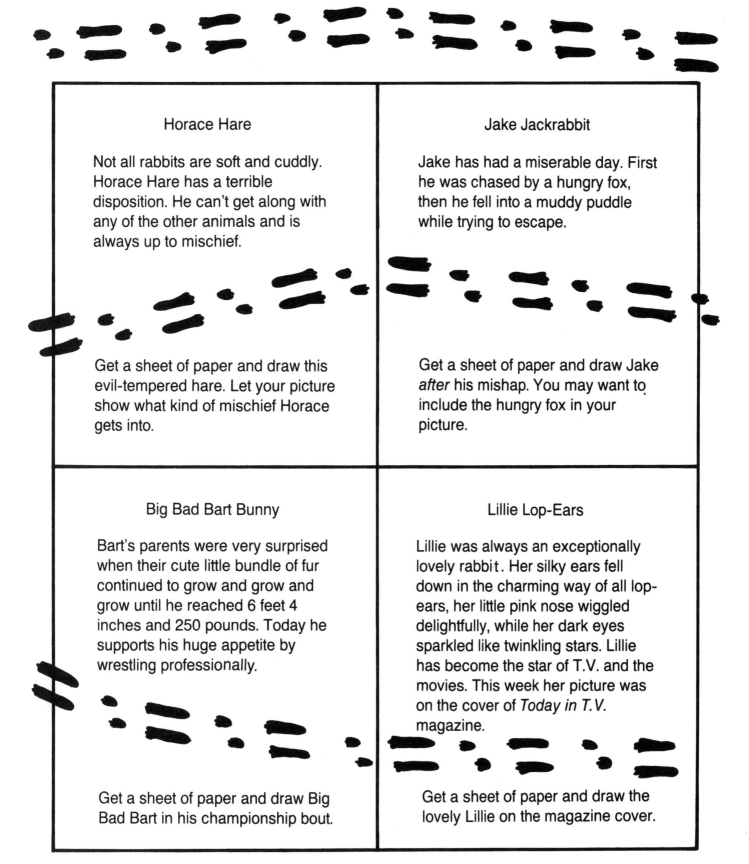

Horace Hare

Not all rabbits are soft and cuddly. Horace Hare has a terrible disposition. He can't get along with any of the other animals and is always up to mischief.

Get a sheet of paper and draw this evil-tempered hare. Let your picture show what kind of mischief Horace gets into.

Jake Jackrabbit

Jake has had a miserable day. First he was chased by a hungry fox, then he fell into a muddy puddle while trying to escape.

Get a sheet of paper and draw Jake *after* his mishap. You may want to include the hungry fox in your picture.

Big Bad Bart Bunny

Bart's parents were very surprised when their cute little bundle of fur continued to grow and grow and grow until he reached 6 feet 4 inches and 250 pounds. Today he supports his huge appetite by wrestling professionally.

Get a sheet of paper and draw Big Bad Bart in his championship bout.

Lillie Lop-Ears

Lillie was always an exceptionally lovely rabbit. Her silky ears fell down in the charming way of all lop-ears, her little pink nose wiggled delightfully, while her dark eyes sparkled like twinkling stars. Lillie has become the star of T.V. and the movies. This week her picture was on the cover of *Today in T.V.* magazine.

Get a sheet of paper and draw the lovely Lillie on the magazine cover.

Seasonal Activities

Little Brown Bunny Bag

Follow these directions to make a bunny bag for yourself or for a little friend.

1. Take a brown lunch bag.

2. Cut out ears.

3. Draw and color:

    pink ears
    black eyes
    black nose
    a little mouth

4. Add: black paper whiskers
    a cotton tail

5. Staple the ears together.
   Open the bag.

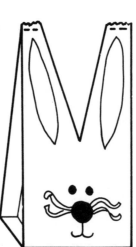

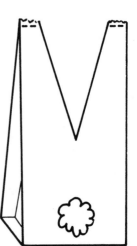

Seasonal Activities

May

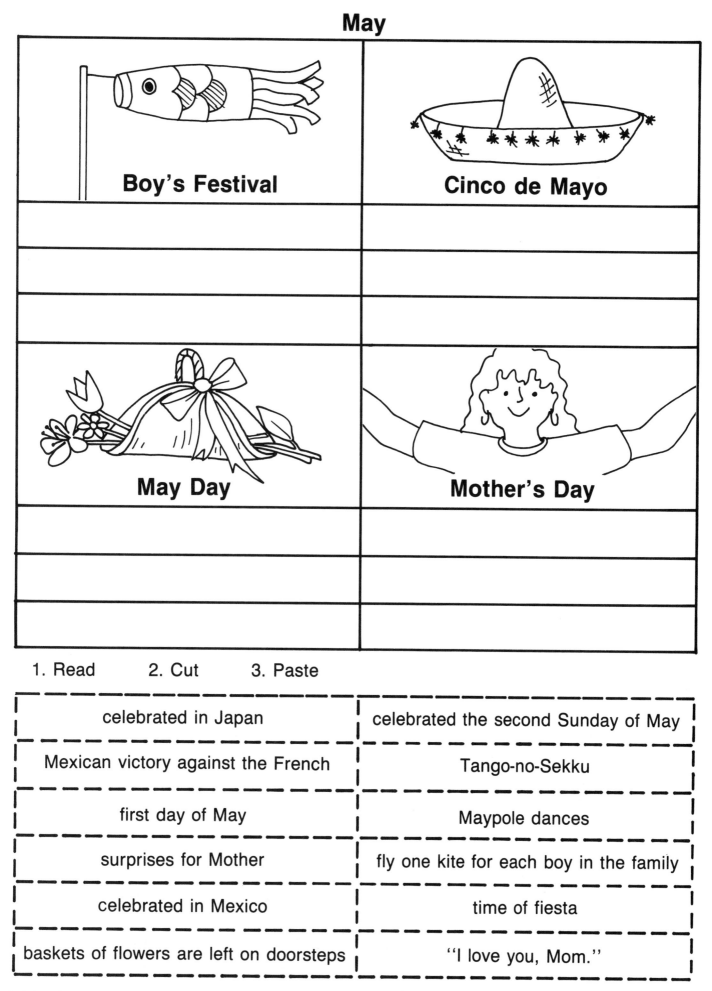

Boy's Festival	Cinco de Mayo
May Day	Mother's Day

1. Read   2. Cut   3. Paste

celebrated in Japan	celebrated the second Sunday of May
Mexican victory against the French	Tango-no-Sekku
first day of May	Maypole dances
surprises for Mother	fly one kite for each boy in the family
celebrated in Mexico	time of fiesta
baskets of flowers are left on doorsteps	"I love you, Mom."

         Seasonal Activities

May

Down

1. a present
2. sons and daughters
3. blooming plants
4. another name for gift
5. the month after April
8. a kind of written greeting

Across

4. May _____ dance
5. Father and _____
6. I _____ you
7. red _____, a kind of flower
9. containers of flowers to leave on doorsteps
10. 24 hours make one _____

Word Box

roses	May	day	gift
card	baskets	love	children
flowers	present	pole	Mother

144

Drawing Fun

Who is out looking for a juicy worm this spring day?
Follow the steps and draw the surprise in the box.

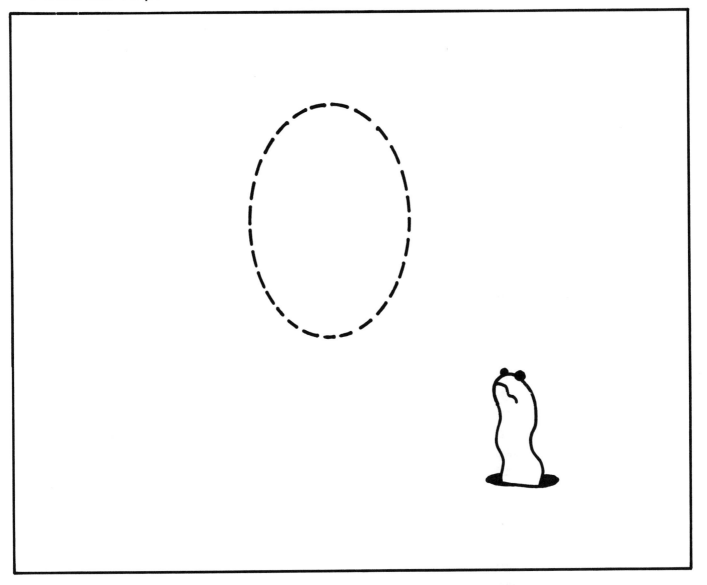

1. Follow the drawing steps.

2. Color the bird blue with an orange bill and feet.
3. Add spring flowers to the garden. Color them your favorite color.

   Seasonal Activities

Spring Bouquet

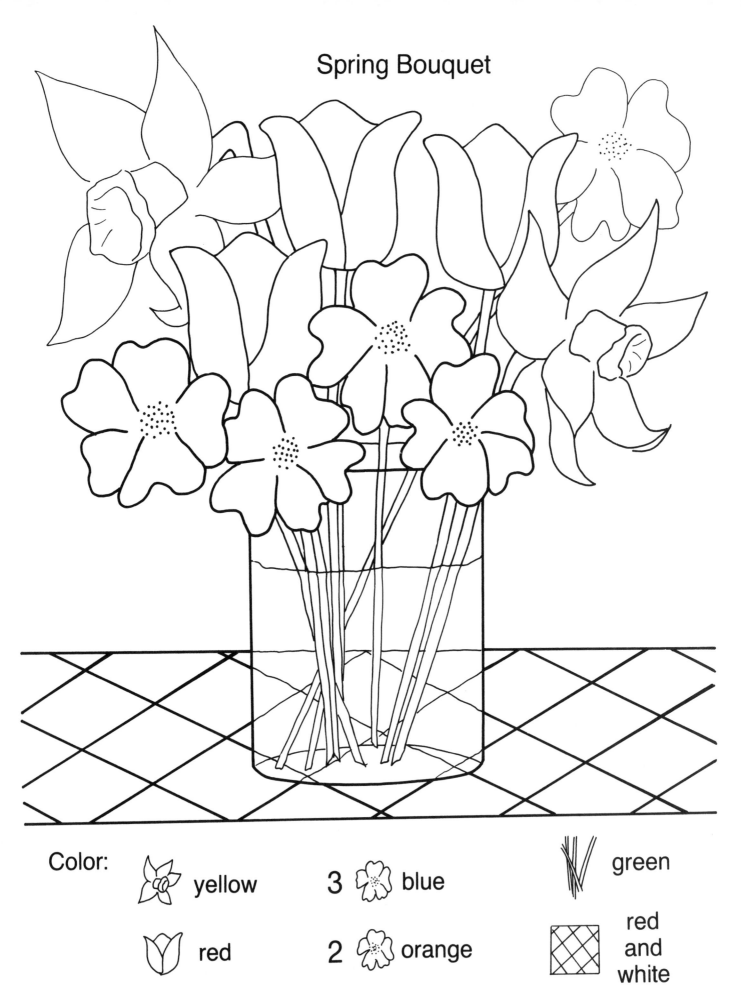

Color:

🌼 yellow   **3** 🌸 blue   🌾 green

🌷 red   **2** 🌸 orange   ▦ red and white

Circle each word in the puzzle as you find it.
You will find words across, down and diagonally.
A few words are written backwards.

May Flowers

```
H G R A S T E R P A N S Y L M
B E G O N I A R E G H U E P T
F R E W L U V C K C R O C U S
D A F F O D I L Z I N N I A L
E N A M P K O I P G B L C O I
J I G T U D L L R A C K A Z T
B U A S C R E A I N C I R O U
F M D F R A T C M P E O N Y L
H M I L E S E Y P O S E A S I
O C O G T A I S O S E O T P P
R E F P T C O I S H M N I O W
C P E T U N I A E J O Y O P E
H B S D B I R D M Z L O N P R
I R I S T N R L J I B V D Y D
D O T B J I H O L L Y H O C K
```

Cross out each word as you find it.

aster	geranium	peony	lily	crocus
begonia	hollyhock	petunia	orchid	daffodil
buttercup	iris	poppy	pansy	daisy
carnation	lilac	zinnia	violet	

Seasonal Activities

Write the answer in each box.

Synonyms

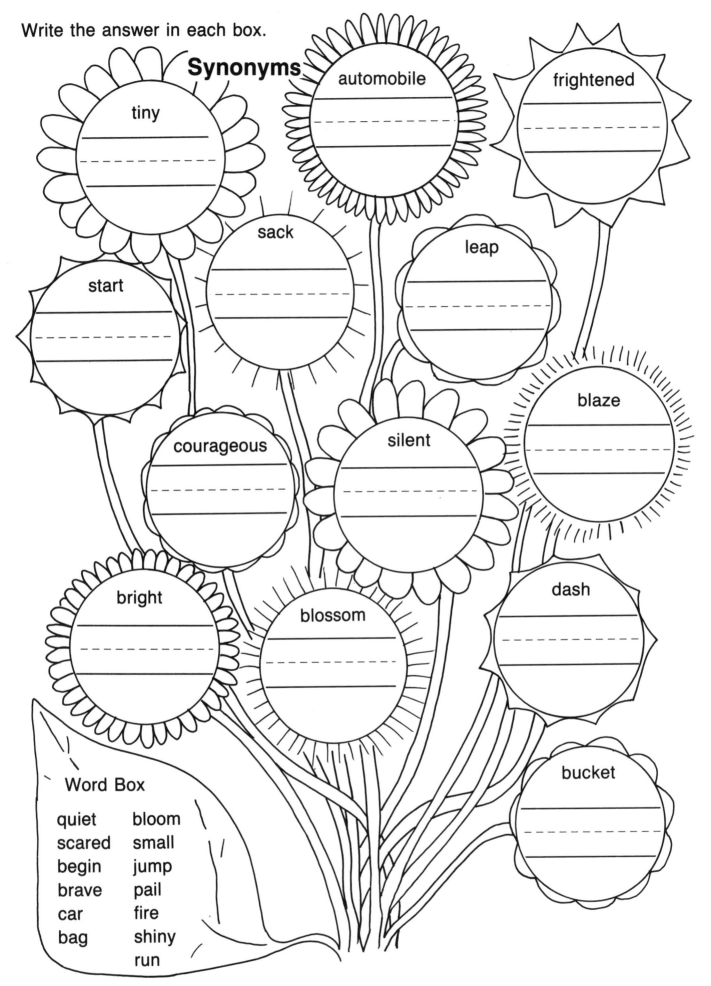

tiny

automobile

frightened

sack

leap

start

blaze

courageous

silent

bright

blossom

dash

bucket

Word Box

quiet	bloom
scared	small
begin	jump
brave	pail
car	fire
bag	shiny
	run

148

Seasonal Activities

Dance Around the Maypole

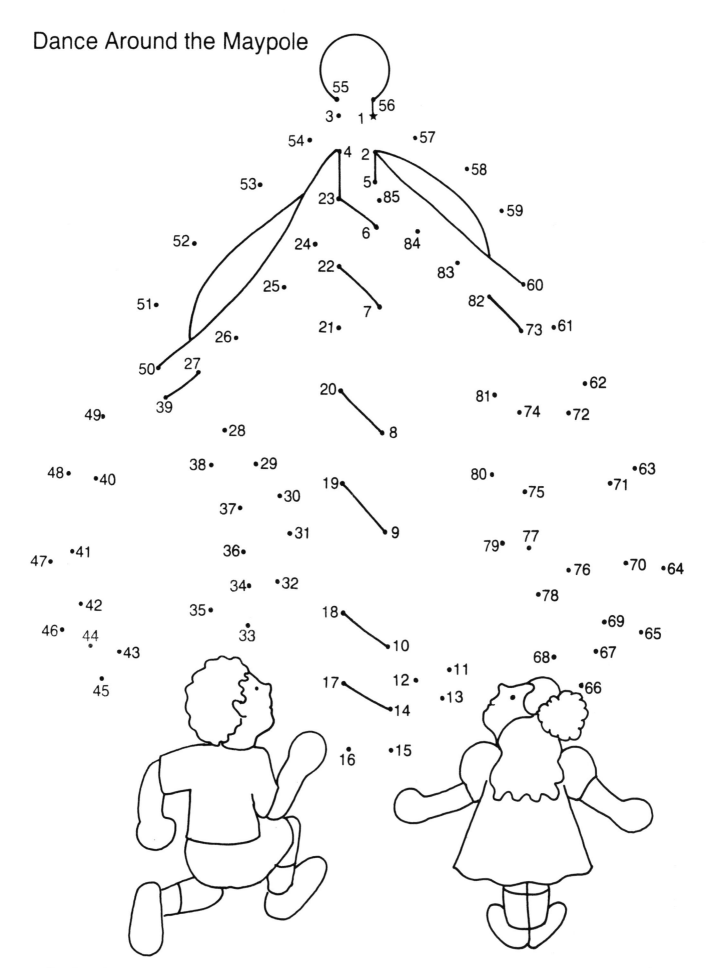

149

Seasonal Activities

Cut and paste the puzzle.

150

_____'s Mother

Draw a picture of your mother inside this frame.

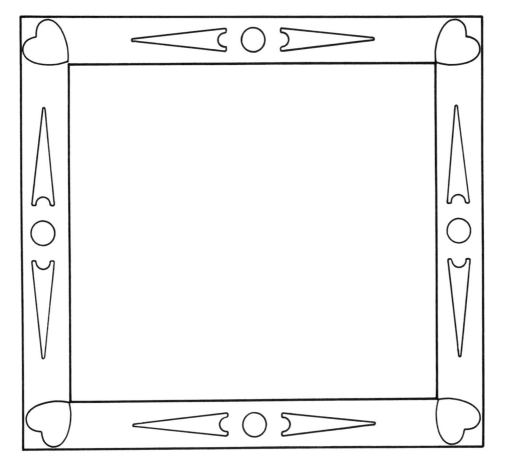

Now, write a description of why she is special.

_____

_____

_____

_____

_____

_____

 Seasonal Activities

A Bear-y Special Mother's Day Card

1. Take a 6" x 9" (15 cm x 22.8 cm) piece of paper.

2. Fold the paper in half.

3. Draw a little bear on the outside.

4. Write this message on the card:

   Outside: This little bear
              is here to say . . .

   Inside: I love you Mother
              EVERY DAY!

5. Sign your name and carry the card home to your own special mother.

                             Seasonal Activities

A Report About _____

your mother's name

Interview your mother to find the information you don't know.

Part 1: A Description

Write a paragraph telling what your mother looks like. Make it clear and complete.

Part 2: Her Childhood

Write one or two paragraphs about when your mother was a girl. Include when and where she was born, what it was like where she lived growing up, her likes and dislikes and any other interesting information about that time in her life.

Part 3: As An Adult

Write one or more paragraphs about your mother now. Include her job, her special interests and talents and what she likes and dislikes now.

Part 4: Write a paragraph explaining why your mother is special.

Copy your report neatly. You may want to include a picture of your mother as a child and as an adult.

 Seasonal Activities

Summer Activities

Seasonal Activities

Name It

	cloth or clothing	city or country	objects in space	food and drink	naming words (nouns)
example **P**	pinafore	Paris	planet	peanut butter	pony
S					
U					
M					
M					
E					
R					

 Seasonal Activities

June	year	The season is: winter summer spring fall

Sunday	Monday	Tuesday	Wednesday	Thursday	Friday	Saturday

1. Write the number for each day in June.
2. There are always _____ days in June.
3. Draw a U.S. flag on Flag Day.
4. Circle in red the first day of summer.
5. Write the name and the number of the last
   day of school. _____
6. Record class birthdays on your calendar.

Turn this paper over and show how you plan to spend the first day of your summer vacation.

 Seasonal Activities

	year	The season is:
July		winter summer spring fall

Sunday	Monday	Tuesday	Wednesday	Thursday	Friday	Saturday

1. Write the number for each day in July.
2. There are always _____ days in July.
3. Draw a firecracker on Independence Day.
4. Which day of the week is the Fourth of July this year? _____
5. How many Sundays are in July? _____
6. Record class birthdays on your calendar.

Turn this paper over and make a picture of your family celebrating Independence Day.

Seasonal Activities

	year	The season is:
August		winter summer spring fall

Sunday	Monday	Tuesday	Wednesday	Thursday	Friday	Saturday

1. Write the number for each day in August.
2. There are always _____ days in August.
3. What day of the week is August 25th?_____
4. Color every Thursday orange.
5. Write the date for each Monday in August.

_____

_____

6. Record class birthdays on your calendar.

Turn this paper over and show one way to keep cool on a hot August day.

June

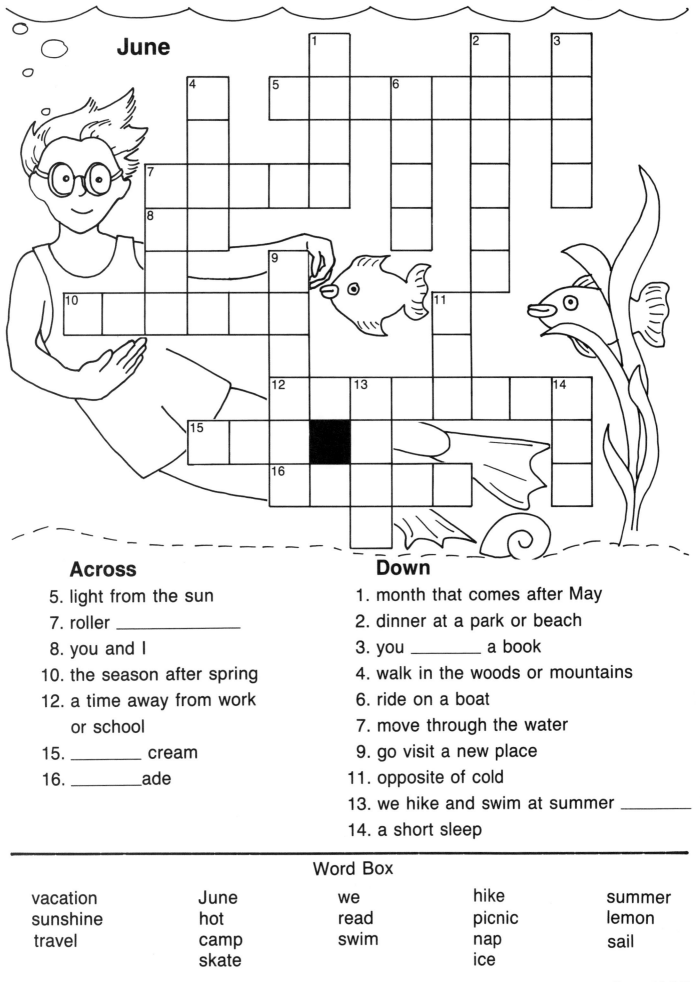

Across

5. light from the sun
7. roller _____
8. you and I
10. the season after spring
12. a time away from work or school
15. _____ cream
16. _____ade

Down

1. month that comes after May
2. dinner at a park or beach
3. you _____ a book
4. walk in the woods or mountains
6. ride on a boat
7. move through the water
9. go visit a new place
11. opposite of cold
13. we hike and swim at summer _____
14. a short sleep

Word Box

vacation	June	we	hike	summer
sunshine	hot	read	picnic	lemon
travel	camp	swim	nap	sail
	skate		ice	

Seasonal Activities

Circle each word in the puzzle as you find it.
You will find words across, down and diagonally.
A few words are written backwards.

Summer Fun

```
B I S U M M E R C V Y E H K V H F B
N C A C L P D X B A F J S C I R L E
R E O F I S H S L C M P U J L U T G
D C E R B Y F P G A H P N I E J K D
N R T M R E A D W T K V S L M O U X
O E V Z A P R S W I M P H Q O S T R
W A I A R W K T E O Y P I C N I C L
U M S L Y A B K Q N E A N D A C G F
O P I R T U I M T R A V E L D B T D
M L T E N B A S E B A L L R E S M C
```

Cross out each word as you find it.

baseball	library	sunshine
bike	picnic	swim
camp	play	travel
fish	read	trip
ice cream	skate	vacation
lemonade	summer	visit

Seasonal Activities

Note: Practice creating acrostics as a group using summer related words before requiring children to do this independently.

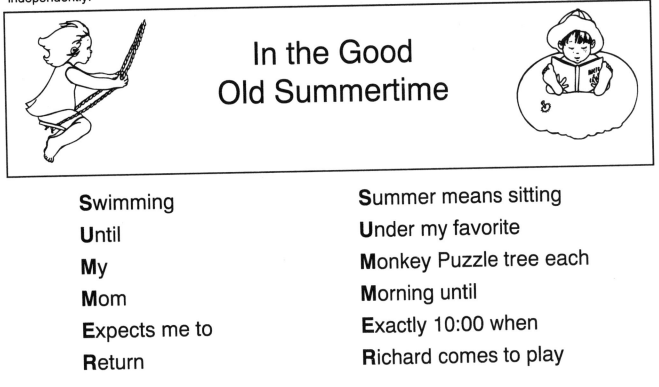

In the Good Old Summertime

Swimming

Until

My

Mom

Expects me to

Return

Summer means sitting

Under my favorite

Monkey Puzzle tree each

Morning until

Exactly 10:00 when

Richard comes to play

Write one word or phrase that begins with each letter of the word SUMMER. Your finished poem must complete a thought about summertime.

S _____

U _____

M _____

M _____

E _____

R _____

Seasonal Activities

By the Sea

color   cut and paste   add

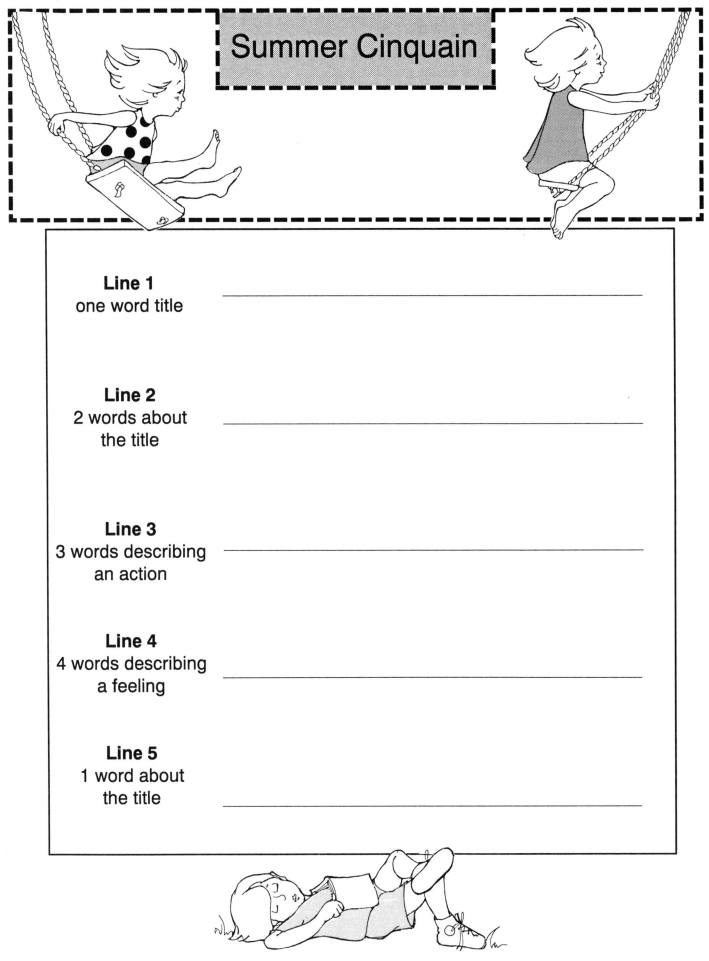

Summer Cinquain

Line 1
one word title
_____

Line 2
2 words about
the title
_____

Line 3
3 words describing
an action
_____

Line 4
4 words describing
a feeling
_____

Line 5
1 word about
the title
_____

Seasonal Activities

Find the Hidden Pictures

In the picnic basket are some great things to eat,
Something crunchy, something salty,
Something nice and sweet.

Seasonal Activities

Write about Summer

1. Cut out the picture.

2. Paste the picture to lined paper.

3. Write a story about it.

_____'s

Picnic Basket

Cranberry
Grape

hsnidawc   lpkiec   urtif

ocieosk   cuiej   tapoot iphsc

Note: Use this form for copying poems, writing letters or creating an original story.

Seasonal Activities

A Summertime Alphabet

Think of words that remind you of summer.
The words may name an object (baseball),
describe something (hot) or name an action (swim).
If you think of more than one word for a letter,
choose the most interesting one to write on your list.

A _____   N _____

B _____   O _____

C _____   P _____

D _____   Q _____

E _____   R _____

F _____   S _____

G _____   T _____

H _____   U _____

I _____   V _____

J _____   W _____

K _____   X _____

L _____   Y _____

M _____   Z _____

Campout Surprise

Where did the bear find a treat?
Connect the dots.
Count by 2s.

Seasonal Activities

Puzzle Fun

Put the puzzle pieces together to find what is hiding here.

1. Cut.
2. Paste to a sheet of paper.
3. Color.

Seasonal Activities

Complete this Funny Face

Seasonal Activities

Summer Adventures

1. Choose a title. Copy it on your writing paper.
2. Put your imagination to work.
3. Write a special story.
4. Illustrate your story.
5. Share it with a friend.

Summer School in Outer Space

Disaster in the Fireworks Factory

Ants at the Picnic

Summer Camp Surprise

Independence Day Parade

Lost in the Woods by S. Sneaker

The Coldest July in History

The Worst (Best) Vacation I Ever Had

Seasonal Activities

Note: Have children cut out the pictures and paste them in sequence to another sheet of paper. Or give child 2 copies of the form on page 174 to use to sequence, then write about cooking popcorn.

How to Pop Popcorn

SALT

HAPPY POP

174 Seasonal Activities

Note: Have children follow these instructions to create bags to use for recycling at home or for collecting litter around the school and neighborhood. Discuss safety if you use plastic bags.

Think Ecologically

Recycling Sacks

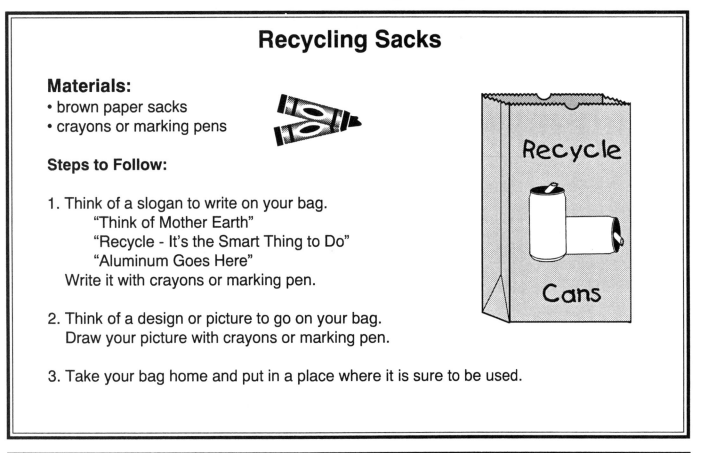

Materials:
- brown paper sacks
- crayons or marking pens

Steps to Follow:

1. Think of a slogan to write on your bag.
    "Think of Mother Earth"
    "Recycle - It's the Smart Thing to Do"
    "Aluminum Goes Here"
   Write it with crayons or marking pen.

2. Think of a design or picture to go on your bag.
   Draw your picture with crayons or marking pen.

3. Take your bag home and put in a place where it is sure to be used.

Trash Bags

Materials:
- plastic garbage bags (or large paper sacks)
- permanent marking pens

Steps to follow:

1. Think of a slogan to go on your trash bag.
    "Clean up Mother Earth"
    "Trash pollution stinks"
    "Pick it up NOW!"
   Write it on your trash bag with permanent marking pens.

2. Take your bag along on a "clean-up" walk around school
   or your neighborhood. Dispose of the trash you collect in
   a proper trash container when you return from your walk.

A Magic Carpet Vacation

Imagine that you have found a wonderful magic carpet. It can carry you anywhere you want to go. Think about these questions, then write about your own <u>Magic Carpet Vacation</u>.

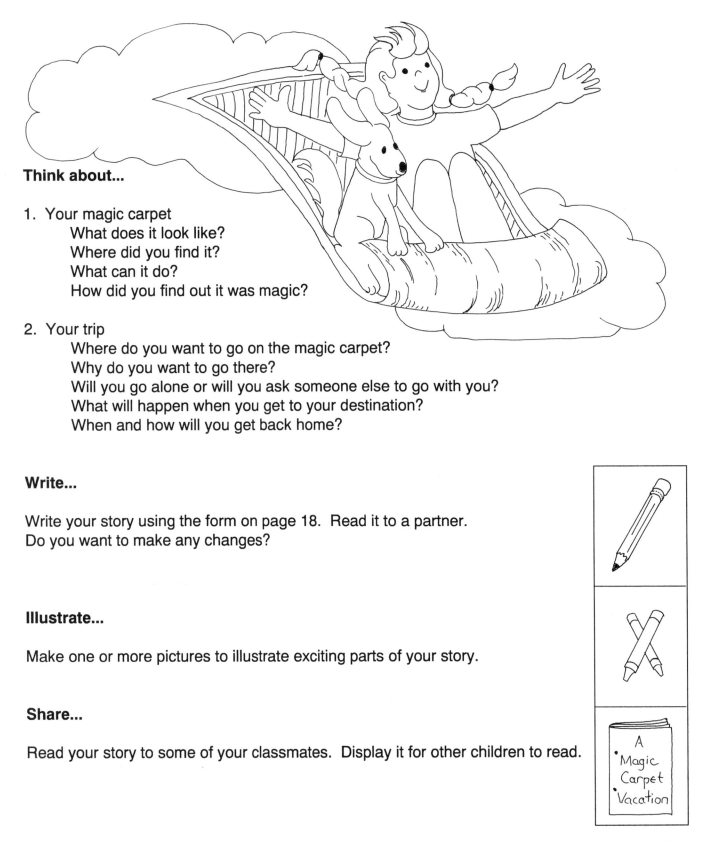

Think about...

1. Your magic carpet
   What does it look like?
   Where did you find it?
   What can it do?
   How did you find out it was magic?

2. Your trip
   Where do you want to go on the magic carpet?
   Why do you want to go there?
   Will you go alone or will you ask someone else to go with you?
   What will happen when you get to your destination?
   When and how will you get back home?

Write...

Write your story using the form on page 18. Read it to a partner.
Do you want to make any changes?

Illustrate...

Make one or more pictures to illustrate exciting parts of your story.

Share...

Read your story to some of your classmates. Display it for other children to read.

Be a Detective

Find a person that can answer "yes" to the question. Have that person sign his/her name on the line.

1. Do you have a baby sister? _____

2. Do you have a pet bird? _____

3. Have you ever been to Disney World? _____

4. Have you ever flown on a plane? _____

5. Can you tap dance? _____

6. Can you speak a language other than English? _____

7. Do you know how to swim? _____

8. Did you go to camp last summer? _____

9. Do you have a summer birthday? _____

10. Do you have hazel eyes? _____

11. Can you ride a horse? _____

12. Can you whistle? _____

13. Are you left-handed? _____

14. Have you ever tasted sushi? _____

15. Were you born in Texas? _____

Summer Fun in Your Own Backyard

Make a list of at least 8 ways to have fun at home.

1. _____

2. _____

3. _____

4. _____

5. _____

6. _____

7. _____

8. _____

Make a list of at least 4 ways to have fun around town.

1. _____

2. _____

3. _____

4. _____

Fisherman's Surprise

Connect the dots.
Count by 4s.

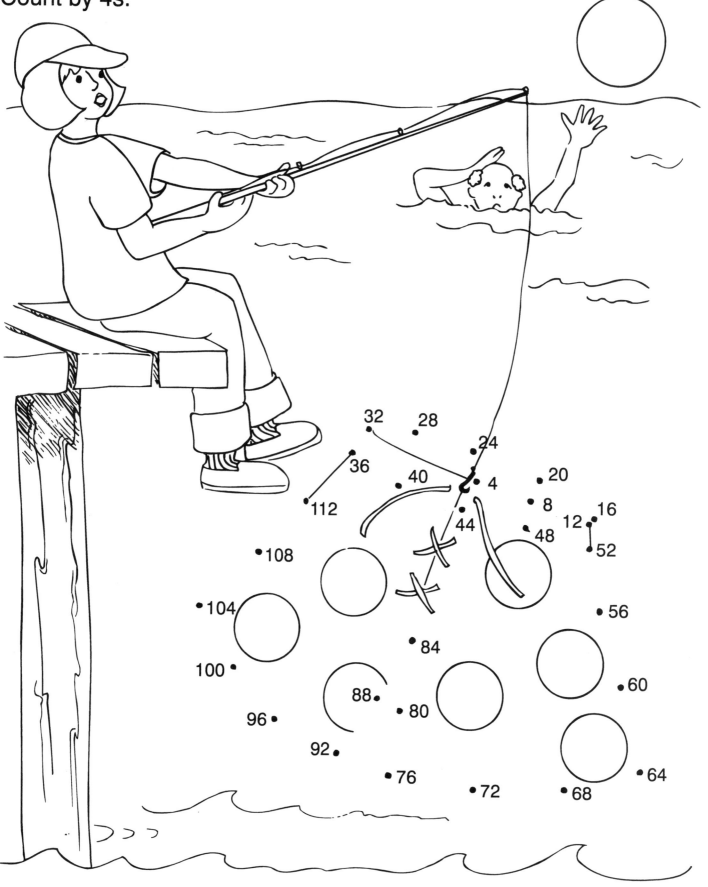

Seasonal Activities

Abbreviations

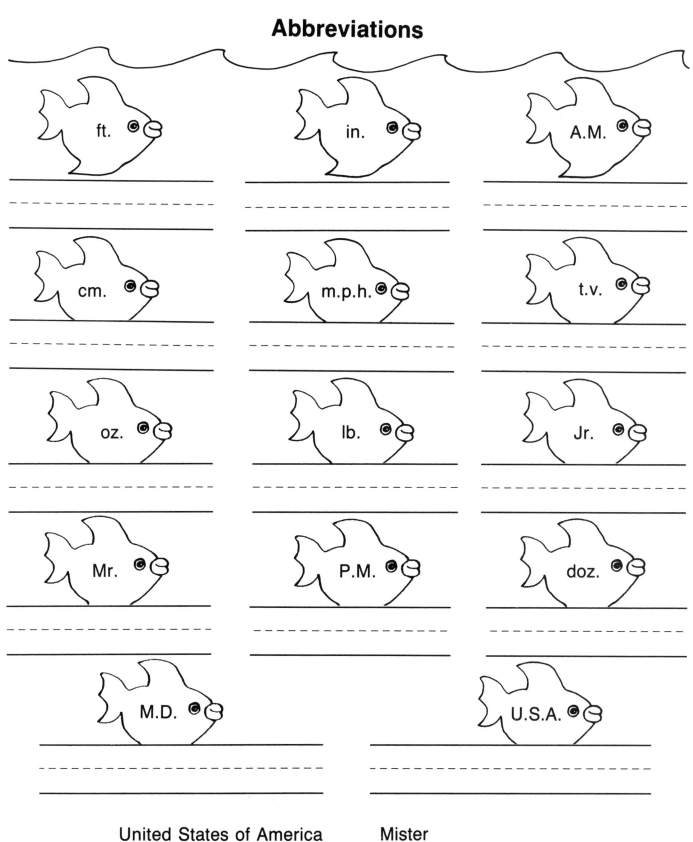

ft.

in.

A.M.

cm.

m.p.h.

t.v.

oz.

lb.

Jr.

Mr.

P.M.

doz.

M.D.

U.S.A.

United States of America
Miles per hour
ounce
Junior
foot
inch
dozen

Mister
after noon
Doctor
centimeter
television
before noon
pound

Seasonal Activities

Cool Treats for a Hot Day

How to make frozen "Juicesicles"

Materials:
- paper cups
- wooden sticks for handles
  (skewers, craft sticks, tongue depressors)
- fruit juice
  (fresh squeezed or make from concentrate)

Steps:
1. Fill each paper cup 2/3 full of fruit juice.
2. Put the cups in a freezer. Check them after a half hour.
3. When ice crystals start to form, put a wooden stick into each cup.
4. Freeze until solid. Take out of the freezer. Peel off the paper and enjoy the juicesicle.

How to make "Frosty Milk"

Materials:
- empty soft drink bottles
- milk
- vanilla flavoring
- sugar
- plastic wrap
- measuring cup
- funnel
- teaspoon

Steps:
1. Put about 1 cup (250 ml) of milk in the measuring cup.
2. Add a drop or two of vanilla flavoring and a teaspoon of sugar to the milk. Stir until mixed.
3. Pour the milk into a bottle. Cover the top with plastic wrap.
4. Place the bottle into a freezer until the milk begins to form crystals. Remove it and drink the delicious cold Frosty Milk.

                   Seasonal Activities

How to Stay Cool
in the Summertime

It is going to be a very hot summer.
Work together to think of 10 ways to stay cool.

1. _____

2. _____

3. _____

4. _____

5. _____

6. _____

7. _____

8. _____

9. _____

10. _____

Now, choose one of the ways on your list.
Demonstrate this method in some way. For example, you could...
- act it out
- draw a detailed picture
- make a model
- write directions
Present the completed project to your classmates.

Seasonal Activities

Up, Up and Away

Finish the balloon.
Who is in the balloon
with Rover?

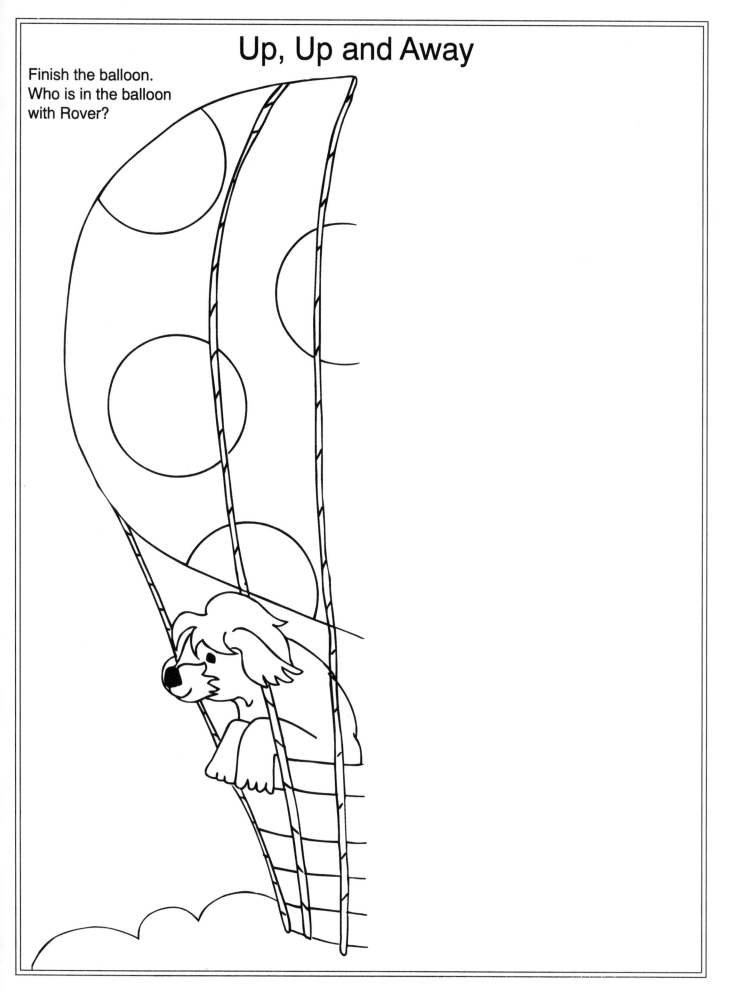

Independence Day - U.S.A.
A Crossword Puzzle

ACROSS

2. explosive devices for making a display of bright lights and loud noises high in the sky
4. freedom from control by others
6. _____ is Independence Day in the U.S.A.
7. a public procession usually having marching bands and floats
9. sounds organized to have rhythm, melody and harmony
10. festive activities for a special occasion

DOWN

1. marching _____ are musical groups in a parade
2. the power to determine your own actions without asking the permission of others
3. a form of communication spoken before an audience
5. vehicles carrying displays in a parade are called
6. pieces of cloth containing special colors or symbols to represent nations
8. we took our lunch to the park in a _____ basket

Seasonal Activities

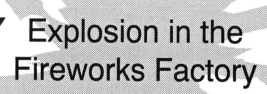

Explosion in the Fireworks Factory

Willie went to bed at his usual time, but he couldn't sleep. He was too excited about tomorrow's celebrations. Independence Day meant a parade, speeches, music, great food and best of all, fireworks!

Suddenly Willie heard sirens and people yelling. He ran to the window and looked out. The sky was filled with flashing lights and bright colors. Matt's Fireworks Plant had exploded.

Write...
a paragraph describing how the sky looked
a story explaining what caused the explosion
a news report about the big disaster

Create...
a drawing or painting of the explosion
a torn paper collage of the colors in the explosion
an etching of fireworks in the night sky

Bonus: Find out if fireworks are allowed in your community. If they are, make a list of rules for fireworks safety. Share your list with your classmates.

Connect the Dots

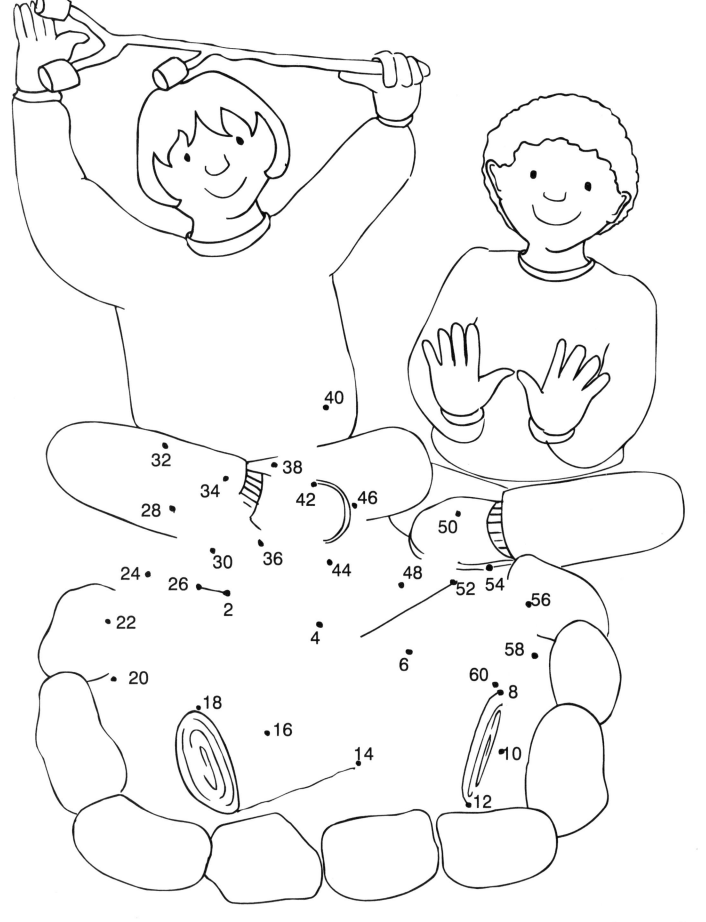

Seasonal Activities

What Did You Do this Summer?

Children are often at a loss as to how to answer this question. Keeping some sort of a log or journal over the summer can help them see how much they really do during their summer vacation. This "log" is kept on calendar pages.

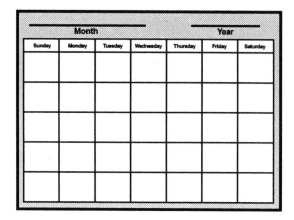

			Month			Year
Sunday	Monday	Tuesday	Wednesday	Thursday	Friday	Saturday

Getting Ready:

Reproduce the calendar form on the following page. Make enough copies for each child to have three (one for each month of summer vacation).

Have children write in the name of the month and the dates on each calendar. This may need to be a guided activity for younger students.

Give each child a sheet of construction paper to fold and use as a folder in which to keep the pages. They may want to draw a summer picture on the front of the folder.

How to Use:

Explain to your students that this is a type of log for keeping track of their summer activities. They are to take a few minutes each day to write or draw a picture of some activity they took part in during the day. This might be something special such as a birthday party or a trip to Disneyland or as simple as playing in the backyard or going to the library.

Brainstorm with students some of the activities they might take part in during the summer.

Model how an event might be written or illustrated in the appropriate box.

Send the folders home on the last day of school.

Seasonal Activities

Note: Reproduce three copies of this calendar form for each child doing the activity.

Month   **Year**

Sunday	Monday	Tuesday	Wednesday	Thursday	Friday	Saturday

Seasonal Activities

On the Beach

Tanya and Luis went to the seashore on Saturday. They found these on the beach.

1. Color the shells.   X the other things.
2. Graph how many there are.

8							
7							
6							
5							
4							
3							
2							
1							

Think about it: Why was it important for Tanya and Luis
to leave the shells and other things at the beach?

         Seasonal Activities

Action Words

1. We ride in the car to the store.

   Yesterday we _____ in the car.

2. I like to swim in the pool.

   Yesterday I _____ in the pool.

3. I hike in the mountains during the summer.

   Yesterday I _____ in the mountains.

4. I read a book today.

   Yesterday I _____ a book.

5. I like to draw with colored pencils.

   Yesterday I _____ a picture.

6. I like to fish in our boat.

   Yesterday I _____ in the lake.

7. I can fly in a glider.

   Yesterday I _____ in a glider.

8. I can throw a ball with my mitt.

   Yesterday I _____ a ball with my mitt.

Fun in the Sun
A Word Search

```
S U M M E R V A C A T I O N C A M P F I R E
U U F A N P A R K H A P P Y A U T O I H S S
N J M R J U M P R O P E I B P G R O S I A W
S U S M I U X L F G L H C A I U I L H K N I
H N A W E E L A I U I O N S C S P X I E D M
I E W N I R N Y S I N O I K E T T E N T C S
N N O I T M T D H D E K C E K I T E G R A U
E S O C E A N I S E B A I T B O A T P A S I
F H D E S A I L M B A C K P A C K O O V T T
R O S C V S U M M E R S C H O O L P L E L H
I R B R A N C H C W E H O L I D A Y E L E A
S T I E N M U U O O F B A S E B A L L G O T
B S K A M A P G T R O T H E M E P A R K N H
E Q E M O V I E A M O S U N G L A S S E S O
E S A N D A L S N S T S W E A T B E A C H T
```

ant	cot	hot	picnic	sweat
August	fan	ice	play	swim
backpack	fish	ice cream	pool	swimsuit
bait	fishing pole	kite	sail	tan
barefoot	friends	July	sandcastle	tent
baseball	frisbee	jump rope	sandals	theme park
basket	fun	June	shorts	travel
beach	guide	line	summer school	trip
bike	happy	map	summertime	van
boat	hat	movie	summer vacation	woods
camp	hike	ocean	sunglasses	worms
campfire	holiday	park	sunshine	
cap	hook			

Seasonal Activities

Put the puzzle pieces together to find who just came out of the woods.

Seasonal Activities

Note: Children will need copies of the jar on this page and the animals on the following page.

A Jar Full of Insects

Cut out the insects and put them in this jar.

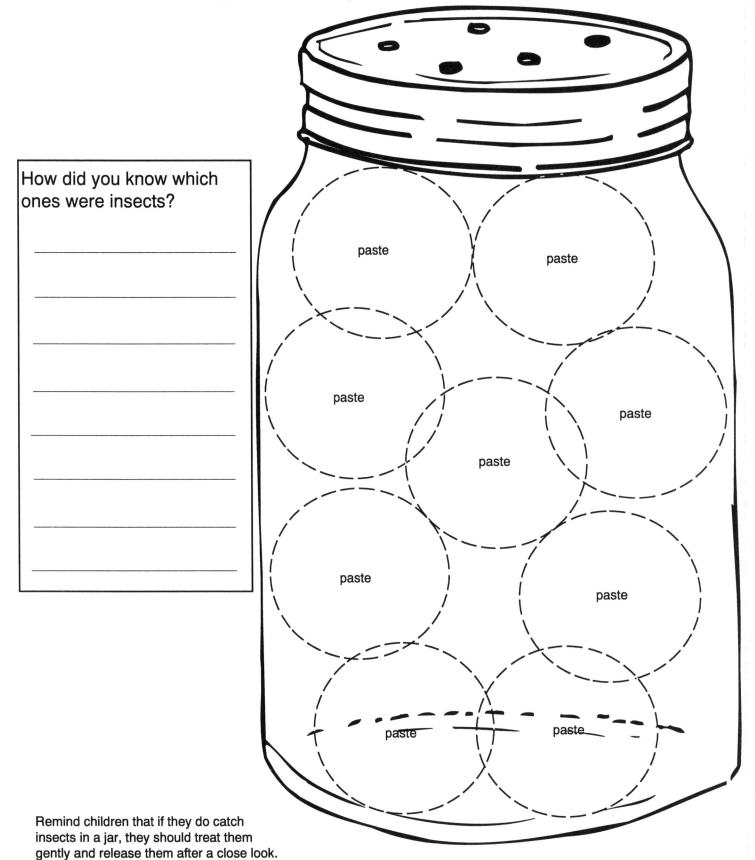

How did you know which ones were insects?

_____

_____

_____

_____

_____

_____

_____

Remind children that if they do catch insects in a jar, they should treat them gently and release them after a close look.

         Seasonal Activities

Find the Insects

 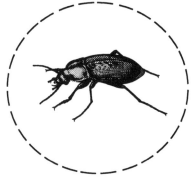 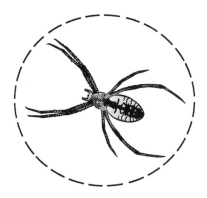

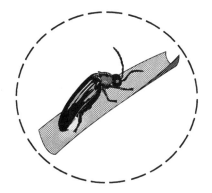 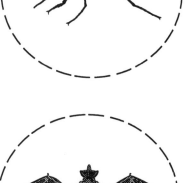 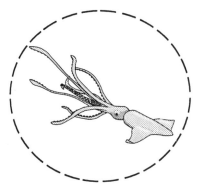

 Seasonal Activities

Note: Have children interview their fathers (or other important male caretaker) to find out information they don't know.

A Report about My Father

Draw him.

Describe him.

My father ______

As a child, my father...

My father is interested in...

My father is special because ______

Flag Day

June 14 is Flag Day in the U.S.A. People fly the Stars and Stripes in front of homes and businesses. People know that this red, white and blue flag stands for the United States of America. The U.S.A. is not the only country that has a red, white and blue flag. Color each of these flags (r-red, b-blue, w-white), then use the code to help you name its country.

a - 26	h - 19	o - 12	u - 6
b - 25	i - 18	p - 11	v - 5
c - 24	j - 17	q - 10	w - 4
d - 23	k - 16	r - 9	x - 3
e - 22	l - 15	s - 8	y - 2
f - 21	m - 14	t - 7	z - 1
g - 20	n - 13		

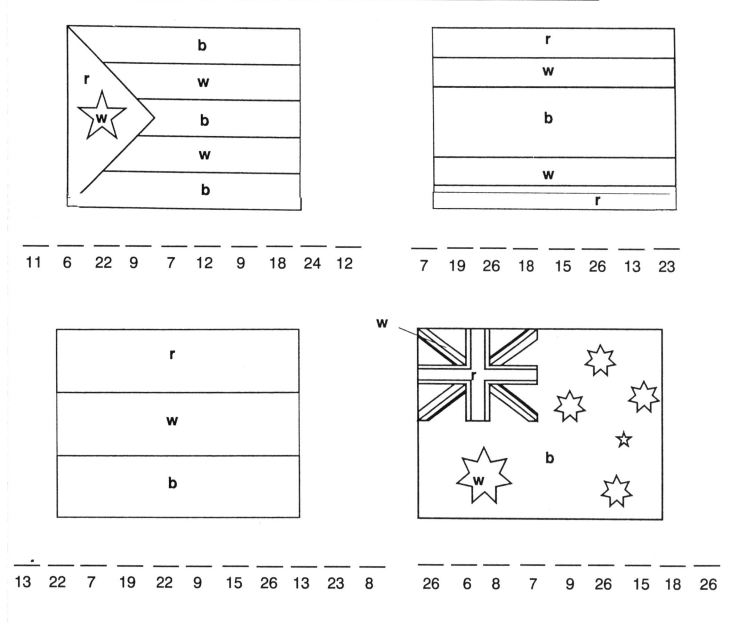

__ __ __ __ __ __ __ __ __ __
11 6 22 9 7 12 9 18 24 12

__ __ __ __ __ __ __ __
7 19 26 18 15 26 13 23

__ __ __ __ __ __ __ __ __ __ __
13 22 7 19 22 9 15 26 13 23 8

__ __ __ __ __ __ __ __ __ __
26 6 8 7 9 26 15 18 26

My Scrapbook of Summer Memories

Materials:
• colored construction paper
• white drawing paper
• hole punch
• yarn for binding pages
• marking pens

Steps to follow:

1. Make your cover.

Decorate a sheet of construction paper as a front cover.

2. Assemble your scrapbook.

Collect the front and back covers and several pieces of white drawing paper. Punch holes in all the sheets.   Lace the pieces together with your piece of yarn.

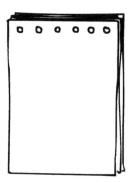

Punch 6 holes.

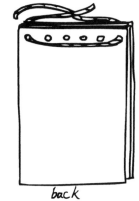

back

front

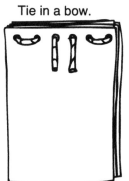

Tie in a bow.

3. Collect summer "memories."

Glue or tape items about your summer on the pages in your scrapbook. These might be...

   postcards

   photographs

   keepsakes from somewhere you visited

   objects you found on walks (shells, feathers, bark...)

or anything else that helps you remember your summer experiences. Label the items. You might even want to write a few sentences about how and where you acquired the object.

                                       Seasonal Activities

Note: You may want to read a story such as *Stringbean's Journey to the Shining Sea* by Vera B. and Jennifer Williams which is about postcards sent home by a child on vacation across the country.

Vacation Postcards

Bring in postcards to share with your students. Encourage them to bring in postcards received by their own families. Display these on a bulletin board with a map. Put a piece of yarn from the postcard to the place from which it came.

Dear Sue,

We are having a great time. The weather is so warm. Wish you could be here.

Your good friend,
Pam

123 The Street, Suite 45
Big City, State, USA 12345

Make Your Own Postcards

Discuss what is found on the front and back of postcards.
What kinds of pictures do you see?
What information is included on the back?
What kinds of messages do people write on postcards?

Materials:
- heavy paper or tag rectangles
- crayons or marking pens

Directions:
1. Think about...
    the place you might visit.
    to whom you might write a postcard.
    what picture you can draw on the front to show where you are.
    what message you will write.

2. Draw the front picture on your card.

3. Address the back and write your message.

Traveling

Unscramble the names of these means of transportation.
Some are for long journeys, some for short journeys and some
for unusual journeys. Draw a line from the word to its picture.

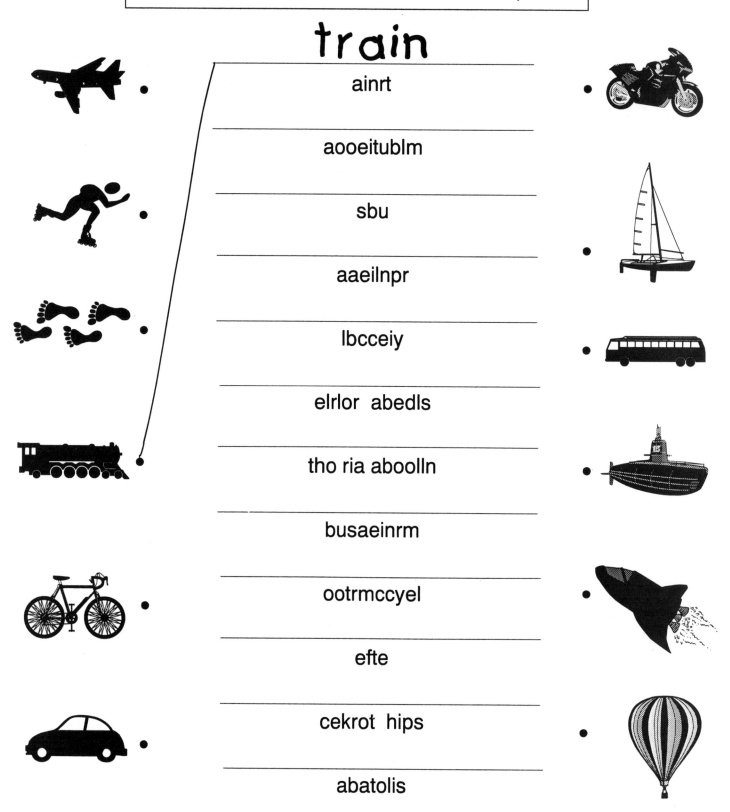

train

ainrt

aooeitublm

sbu

aaeilnpr

lbcceiy

elrlor abedls

tho ria aboolln

busaeinrm

ootrmccyel

efte

cekrot hips

abatolis

 # Ways to Get There

	Things I like about it.	Things I don't like about it.	I have traveled this way before

Note: Brainstorm all the types of activities, exciting and disastrous, that might happen at summer camp. Give children a copy of this form and set their imaginations to work as they practice writing friendly letters.

News from Camp

Touring North America

Use the code to help you find the names of these special places to visit on holiday.

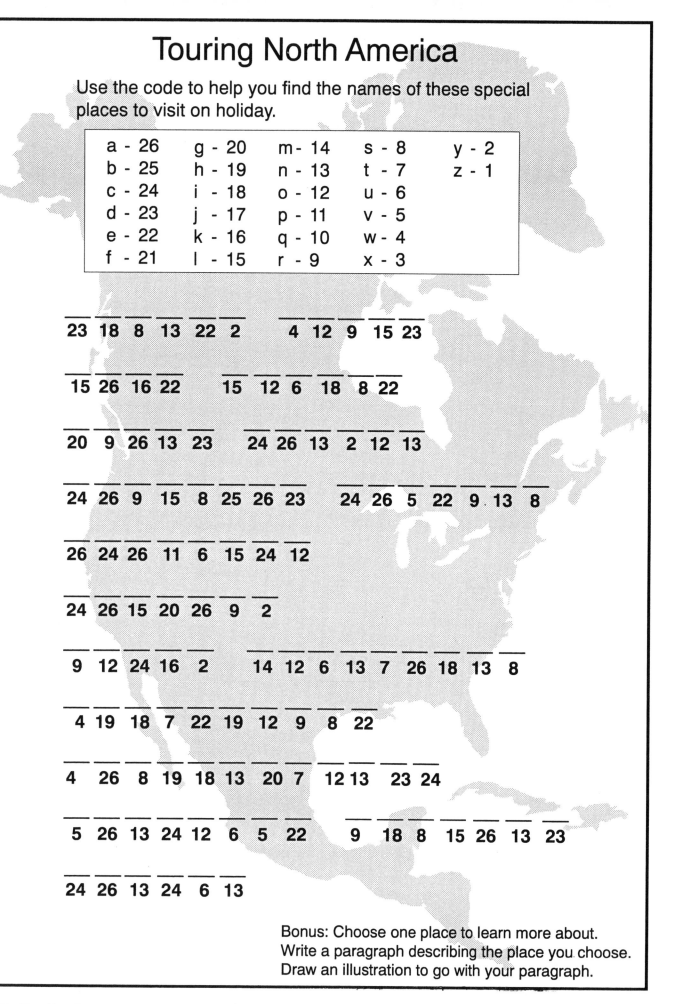

a - 26	g - 20	m - 14	s - 8	y - 2
b - 25	h - 19	n - 13	t - 7	z - 1
c - 24	i - 18	o - 12	u - 6	
d - 23	j - 17	p - 11	v - 5	
e - 22	k - 16	q - 10	w - 4	
f - 21	l - 15	r - 9	x - 3	

23 18 8 13 22 2   4 12 9 15 23

15 26 16 22   15 12 6 18 8 22

20 9 26 13 23   24 26 13 2 12 13

24 26 9 15 8 25 26 23   24 26 5 22 9 13 8

26 24 26 11 6 15 24 12

24 26 15 20 26 9 2

9 12 24 16 2   14 12 6 13 7 26 18 13 8

4 19 18 7 22 19 12 9 8 22

4 26 8 19 18 13 20 7 12 13 23 24

5 26 13 24 12 6 5 22   9 18 8 15 26 13 23

24 26 13 24 6 13

Bonus: Choose one place to learn more about.
Write a paragraph describing the place you choose.
Draw an illustration to go with your paragraph.

Seasonal Activities

Pop-Up Picnic Basket

Brainstorm to create a list of all the types of items you would pack in a picnic basket (food and non-food items).

Model the sentence format to be used on the page.
>   I have crunchy green pickles in my picnic basket.
>   I have yummy peanut butter and jelly sandwiches in my picnic basket.
>   I have soft, sweet marshmallow cookies in my picnic basket.
>   I have a red and white checked napkin in my picnic basket.

Demonstrate how the pop-up pages are made and how they are put together into the picnic basket cover.

Materials:
- pop-up form (page 205)
- picnic basket cover form (page 206)
- pencils
- crayons
- glue and scissors

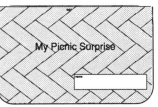

My picnic _____

Directions:

1. Have children complete the writing form.

2. They then draw illustrations of the items in their basket on the small drawing form. Cut and fold the pop-up form as shown. Cut out and paste the illustration to the pop-up form.

3. Finally they color their basket "cover" forms and paste in their pop-up pages as shown here.

Seasonal Activities

Pop-Up Steps:

fold 2

fold 1

paste

fold 2

My picnic

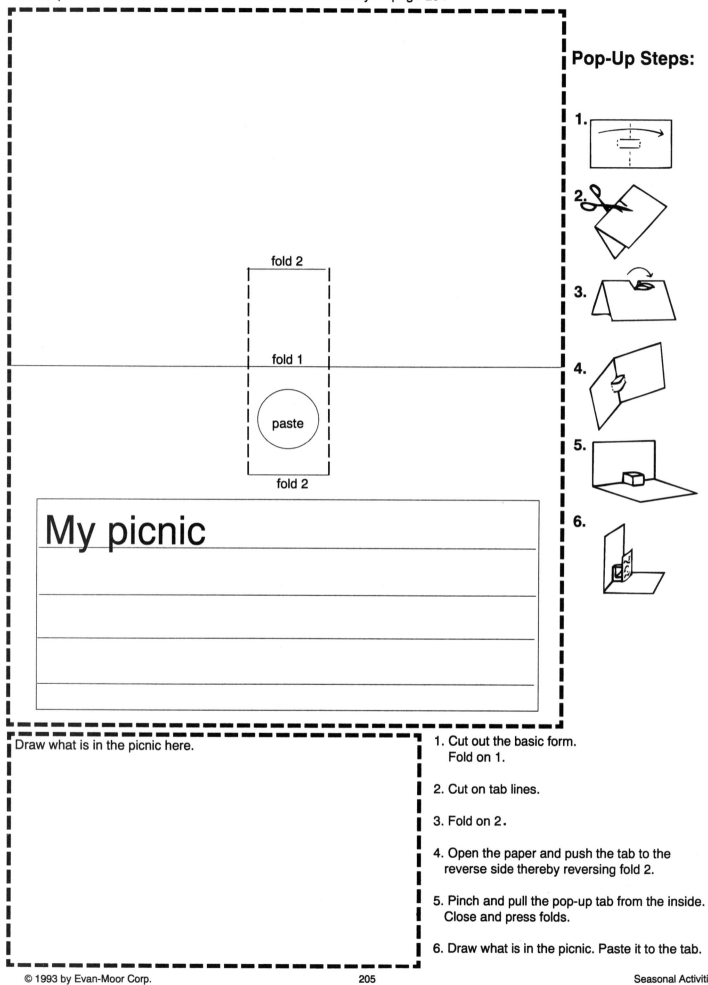

Draw what is in the picnic here.

1. Cut out the basic form.
   Fold on 1.

2. Cut on tab lines.

3. Fold on 2.

4. Open the paper and push the tab to the reverse side thereby reversing fold 2.

5. Pinch and pull the pop-up tab from the inside.
   Close and press folds.

6. Draw what is in the picnic. Paste it to the tab.

Seasonal Activities

Note: Reproduce this form to use with the Picnic Basket activity on page 204

The Picnic Basket
Pop-Up Cover

cut

fold

My Picnic Surprise

name

Follow the directions to finish this picture

__ Color the pond blue.

__ Make six fish in the pond.

__ Draw a canoe on the pond. Color it red. Put a girl in it.

__ Draw three tall pine trees next to the pond.

__ Make a tent by the pond. Color it brown.

__ Put a campfire in front of the tent.

__ Make three people sitting near the campfire.

 Seasonal Activities

Let's Have a Party!

Your challenge is to plan a great party for summer. It can be for something specific such as Father's Day, Independence Day or someone's summer birthday or just for fun such as a barbecue, pizza party or sleep-over. Read through all of these directions before you begin.

Assign someone in your group to take notes as you discuss plans, and assign someone else in the group to collect the materials you need to do each part.

Planning:

1. Decide what type of party you are going to give, how many people are going to be invited, where the party will be held and when it will be held.

2. Make a list of the food you will serve.
   Figure out how much you will need and how much it will cost.

3. Describe the decorations you will put out.
   Figure out what you will need to make them or where you will buy them.
   Figure out how much they will cost.

4. Decide what entertainment you will have.
   Will you have music? If so, what kind?
   Will you play games? If so, what?

5. Design an invitation that shows the type of party you are giving.
   Include when and where the party will take place.

6. Plan a work list for your group for the day of the party. Who will...
   cook the food
   greet people at the door
   take care of the entertainment
   clean-up after the party